# You're The Elephant Man

# You're The Elephant Man

### If you're still alive after two weeks, you're permanent

*Frank Kinsey Evans*

Writer's Showcase
presented by *Writer's Digest*
New York  San Jose  Lincoln  Shanghai

You're The Elephant Man
If you're still alive after two weeks, you're permanent

Writer's Showcase
presented by *Writer's Digest*
an imprint of iUniverse.com, Inc.

For information address:
iUniverse.com, Inc.
620 North 48th Street, Suite 201
Lincoln, NE 68504-3467
www.iuniverse.com

ISBN: 0-595-12500-X

Printed in the United States of America

# Dedication

This book is dedicated to the following people. There were many others who were instrumental in forming the final product, but these people were critical.

First, I dedicate this book to my wife, Yvonne, without whom this book would still be just stories told around the dinner table.

Second, I dedicate this book to my son, Larry. I am sorry your mornings, sleeping in on your day off, were disturbed by the clatter of my printer.

Third, I dedicate this book to my parents, Sally and Tom Evans, without whom I would not have been possible.

Fourth, I dedicate this book to Tommy "Mac" Harrell, who kept my computer working, and who provided a pat on the back when I needed it.

And finally, I dedicate this book to Blake Rutland, who's life was taken from him, long before he reached his full potential.

# Epigraph

Look at the behemoth, which I made along with you and which feeds
on grass like an ox.
What strength he has in his loins, what power in the muscles of his belly!
His tail sways like a cedar; the sinews of his thighs are close-knit.
His bones are tubes of bronze, his limbs like rods of iron.
He ranks first among the works of God, yet his Maker can approach
him with his sword.
The hills bring him their produce, and all the wild animals play nearby.
Under the lotus plants he lies, hidden among the reeds in the marsh.
The lotuses conceal him in their shadow; the poplars by the stream
surround him.
When the river rages, he is not alarmed; he is secure, though the Jordan
should surge against his mouth.
Can anyone capture him by the eyes, or trap him and pierce his nose?"

Job 40: 15-24; The Bible (NIV)

# Contents

# Foreword

This is a book about my years in the animal business. It is a series of vignettes put together rather randomly. Because it may be somewhat difficult to follow the chronology, let me give you some background information on dates, times, places, and people.

I started in the animal business in march of 1972 at the new Lion Country Safari park near Jonesboro, Georgia, just south of Atlanta. The park was still under construction when I arrived, and it opened for the 1972 summer season. We attempted to stay open all year round, but we had many days in the winter when we had to close the park due to weather or low attendance.

The park was designed with one large hoof stock section which wrapped around a man-made lake. In the lake were islands where representatives from the four great ape families were displayed. The lake was adjacent to the central entertainment complex and parking lot. At the east end of the Hoofstock section were the Cheetah/Rhino section and the Lion/Barbary ape section.

Visitors would drive their cars along the road which meandered around through the park, and could take as much or as little time as they wanted to sit and watch the animals. There were fences between the sections and guards stationed on the gates to keep animals where they were supposed to be. There were also guards in Jeeps who either sat and watched animals, as in the Lion section, or patrolled their sections, as in the Hoofstock section. I was usually out on foot in the Hoofstock section with my elephants.

The people driving through the park were instructed, in several fashions, that they were to keep their windows closed, and never leave their vehicles. These instructions were frequently ignored. There were serious accidents at the other Lion Countrys, but we were fortunate not to have had any of those kinds of tragedies. We did have some close calls, however.

Some of the people I remember from those days at lion country include Richard "Gus" Gustafson, our Chief Game Warden; Melvin Richardson, the primate man, a dark brooding smart fellow who left Lion country to go to Veterinary school. Rick Aiken, a "good old" local boy who took care of the cheetahs and rhinos, and lost the end of his thumb doing it, and who was given the Senior Ranger position. Nick Reindl, tall thin and soft spoken, who was the hoof stock man and assistant Senior ranger.

Jimmy Lee, the cat man, a tall, good-looking young man who had jet black hair already sprinkled with gray. Jimmy Lee was a man you definitely wanted for a friend—not an enemy. It was Jimmy Lee who introduced me to the delightful treat of date-nut bread with cream cheese. Beth Teeple, a dear friend with whom I worked at Lion Country (and would work with at the Wildlife Preserve), who took care of Cuddle Corner. It was she who spread the word about me and got me hired by the American Broadcasting Company.

Our veterinarian was a Dr. Mort Silberman. He was a local man who was not trained in exotic animals but since 1972 has become one of the country's experts. And, of course, Bill York, big, red, man, whose right arm doesn't straighten all the way, as a result of a bullet wound to the elbow he got in some uprising in Africa. He was the zoological director of all of the Lion Country Safaris. He was the man who hired me as we sat around a campfire in Africa.

I stayed at Lion Country for two years and in March of 1974, I was hired by the American Broadcasting Company to work at a drive-thru park they were building near Mitchellville, Maryland, just east of Washington D. C.. The name of the park was the Wildlife Preserve. It was here I got to know Tom Cavanaugh, then vice-president of ABC Scenic and Leisure division. Tom and I became great friends and worked together for many more years. Tom's boss was a Mr. John Campbell. (Hi John, Larry told me you spoke well of me, thanks.)

Prior to going to Maryland, I spent three months living in Ocala, Florida, taking care of animals housed at Silver Springs, "Home of the World Famous Glass Bottom Boats," and in a compound near Clairmont, Florida. During these three months I worked with Ken Parker at Clairmont, Ken was a short, trim, fellow who loved life and his cats. Ken would soon join me at The Wildlife Preserve and we would become the Senior Rangers there. I also met and worked with Leon Cheatom at Silver Springs. Leon is the hardest working man I have ever met. He had worked at Silver Springs since he was just a kid and knew all of its nooks and crannies. I was to work with Leon for many more years, but didn't know it at the time.

In June of 1974, I moved to the Wildlife Preserve in Mitchellville, Maryland. I spent several weeks living in a hotel, while we settled in and prepared the park for opening. The Wildlife Preserve was shaped like an extended tear drop. You entered the pointed end and entered the parking lot. The entertainment section was between the parking lot and the animal sections which took up most of the round end of the tear drop shape.

The first year of opening the Wildlife Preserve was a drive-thru park like Lion Country. But the second year the company purchased these big trams, air conditioned bus-like things with large windows all around. These trams worked, off and on. People would park their cars and have to tour the animal habitats while inside the trams. The trams were tandem affairs and held quite a few people. However, there was usually always a line when the park was crowded. Lots of people were dissatisfied with the trams because they couldn't set their own pace through the park. People wanted to stop when they wanted to stop, and see what they wanted to see for as long as they wanted to see it. The wildlife preserve was only open during the warmer months and was closed for the winter.

The drive-thru component of the Wildlife Preserve was a road which took a horseshoe-like path and wound around and through the animal sections. You entered the animal sections on the East side of the entertainment section and began your journey by passing through the North American Hoofstock section I. Like Lion Country, there were gates between sections, and guards on most of the gates.

One thing we did differently at The Wildlife Preserve was to have cattle guards at some of the gates in an attempt to keep animals in, or out, of the section. These cattle guards were made of concrete and were constructed like a large storm grate, with laterals separated by holes that were supposed to make the animals unsure enough of their footing so that they would not cross them. The theory was sound, but the cattle guards were designed for cattle. Some of the animals we had were quite comfortable walking across the tops of the laterals and some had feet so big that the slatting effect didn't bother them. Also, we had animals that could easily jump over the entire structure. These cattle guards didn't work as well as we had hoped and we ended up using more gate guards than we had anticipated.

Since we had different problems to solve at the predator and baboon sections, we installed electric cattle guards at those spots. These were slat-like metal structures which had a slight electric charge running through them. When the animal would touch two adjacent slats, it would get a mild electric shock, which regularly pulsed through the metal. Theoretically, this would convince the animals not to cross the cattle guard. These worked about as well as the other cattle guards.

After a short drive through the North American Hoofstock section I, which had a beautiful old chestnut tree which had somehow survived the blight of many years ago, you entered the Bear and Wolf section. Following the Bear and Wolf section, was the North American Hoof Stock section II. From there you entered the South American hoof stock section which curved around and led into the small Australian section. The Australian section led into the Rhino/Baboon section.

I use the name Rhino/Baboon loosely because the Baboons actually stayed pretty much wherever they wanted, and the rhinos spent most of their time in the Elephant section. After the Rhino section came the elephant section. The elephants, rhinos, and baboons had their holding pens in the lower part of the rhino/baboon section, and I would walk the elephants back into that area at the end of the day.

Leaving the Elephant section, you went into the African Hoofstock section, a large section which gave way to the Lion section. The Lion section was the last part of the drive-thru and was directly adjacent to the entertainment area. Overlooking the whole park, at the top of a hill, was an old empty mansion built in the 1700's, and surrounded by a group of very old oak trees. The public wasn't allowed up to the mansion, but they could see it from the animal sections and from the entertainment area.

My boss, for a while, at the Wildlife preserve was Ron Bugosh, Ron had been a sea mammal trainer and had survived a bite to the stomach by an elephant seal. He was replaced by a burly man from New York by the name of Bob McLaughlin. Bob was one of those guys with a high profile, you always knew when he was around. Milton Teirney was our cat man. Milton was, and, I assume, still is, into photography. The last I saw of Milton, he as working for the National Zoo in Washington, D.C..

Another employee who worked for the National Zoo (with the Pandas!) was Morna Holden. Morna was a good friend and good animal person. Some of the other good people who worked at the Wildlife Preserve were Norma Corrado, Gary Maelstrom, Ken Parker, and Beth Teeple. Our veterinarian was Mitch Bush from the National Zoo. I loved working with Mitch about as much as anything. A lot of people had a hard time getting along with Mitch, but I never did. He was a master at what he did, and I learned a great deal from him. (I doubt if you remember me, Mitch, but thanks for the memories.)

After two years at the wildlife preserve, ABC decided to cut its losses and shut the park down. Bob McLaughlin and I were transferred to Silver Springs so that we could beef up the Jungle Cruise ride there. We developed the current Jungle Cruise ride at Silver Springs which has exotic animals along the banks of a canal on the Silver River

After about a year, Bob left and the company put Andy Kukulous in charge. Andy had been in charge of the Ross Allen Reptile institute since Ross Allen left. Andy left to go to Cypress Gardens and I finally got my chance to run a park. Tom Cavanaugh put me in charge of the wildlife area first, then gave me the responsibility for the reptile institute and the deer park.

At Silver Springs, I developed a core of employees who worked hard and did everything they could for the animals and the park. Blake Rutland, who tragically died in an automobile accident at the age of 22. Chris Gill, who is probably going to be, or is already, a famous author/designer/creator. Al Parker (Al, look out for that camel). Steve Shurter who went on to greater things at the Metro Zoo in Miami. And last but not least Joanne Zeliff, whose gentle nature made her a natural in the animal business, and who is, at this writing, still at Silver Springs, keeping things going the way we set them up those many years ago.

I stayed with ABC at Silver Springs till march of 1982 when I decided to try my hand at running a park that Jim Fowler was building on the site of the old Wildlife Preserve in Mitchellville, Maryland. They called their park Wildworld. At Wildworld I met two of the most unique individuals I have ever met, Ted Svertesky and Joe Frisco. These two elephant trainers were to have a significant impact in my life. I truly miss them. Jim Fowler soon left the park, and the management and I had significant philosophical differences. So, after working there for four months, seven days a week, from sunup to sunset and beyond, I left Wildworld and came back to Ocala, Florida for a rest.

It was during this rest that I decided to try to go back to college and become a veterinarian. At about the time I had made this decision Mr. Roland Lindeman called me. Mr. Lindeman was the grandfather of the zoo business in this country, and owned and operated the Catskill Game farm in New York, as well as the Rare Animal Survival Center in Ocala, Florida. Mr. Lindeman wanted to come and talk to me about a job. I tell you, when Mr. Lindeman asked if he could come to my house, and talk to me about a job, I was flabbergasted. This man was one of the most respected men in the exotic animal business, and he was coming to see me.

He offered me the job of supervising the Rare Animal Survival Center in Ocala, Florida. This was an offer that, had I received it at any other time in my career, I would have jumped at. But I had made up my mind to go back to school. Mr. Lindeman was so gracious that he offered me a job where I could work whenever I could, and set my own schedule. I did jump at that opportunity. The Rare Animal Survival Center had over two million dollars worth of rare and endangered species and the public wasn't allowed in. It was kind of like having your own private zoo to take care of. I worked there until I started commuting to Gainesville to go to the University of Florida.

The pressures of school, work, and the commute, were too much, and I officially left the animal business in June of 1983. I never did get into veterinary school, although my grades and credentials were extremely high. But, it was a blessing in disguise. After taking all the course work required in a masters degree in wildlife ecology, I left the university to teach chemistry and ecology at Lake Weir High School near my home in Ocala, Florida. I am currently teaching chemistry at Forest High School in Ocala.

There were many other people I didn't mention who were involved in the many places I worked, and to them I apologize. To the people I have mentioned, I hope you have fared as well as I have. You still live fondly in my memory.

# Chapter 1: Moja

I first met Moja in the spring of 1972. Rather long-legged and thin, she wasn't what you would call a beauty. Her skin was really wrinkled and very gray. She had this long, thin face and had very sparse hair all over her body. Although she was about seven feet tall, she only weighed about 4000 pounds. Oh, by the way, Moja was my first elephant. Moja means first in Swahili.

My first job in the animal business was to care for some African White Rhinoceroses at the Lion Country Safari park just south of Atlanta, Georgia. I had to feed them and clean up after them. While I was taking care of the Rhinos one day, Bill York, the big Afrikaner who had given me this job while we sat around a campfire just outside the boundaries of Kruger National Park in South Africa, approached me and asked whether or not I'd like to be the elephant man, not *the* Elephant Man, the *elephant* man, (not surprisingly, people who take care of elephants are called elephant men). I had never seen an elephant from closer than thirty feet before. While I was wondering whether the job required me to wear a turban and a loin cloth, Bill York said "You're the elephant man. If you're still alive after two weeks, you will be the permanent elephant man."

Bill said, "Hop in the Jeep." and we drove up to the elephant barn. I got out of the Jeep and was looking around when I got this funny feeling. I turned around slowly, like some idiot in a bad spooky movie, and sure enough, here was a nightmare staring right at me.

Inside the elephant barn was the biggest animal I had ever seen (at least it seemed so at the time). It had its ears spread out like two great sails and a nose that must have been seven feet long. My curiosity got the best of me and I slowly approached the barn.

I was about twelve feet from the gate when I was introduced to the sound an elephant makes. Tarzan movies aside, this was a noise that could decalcify your spinal column. Needless to say, the noise stopped me dead in my tracks. But when Moja (not her name at the time) charged the front gate of the elephant barn, crashing into it like a runaway freight train, I was no longer frozen in my tracks. I jumped and ran so fast, I nearly left my shoes.

Bill was nearly falling down laughing. I asked him, in a somewhat shaky voice, "what's so funny?" He just said "Well, now that you are introduced, I'll leave you." Bill then hopped in his Jeep and drove off, laughing all the way, leaving me to my thoughts. And what thoughts they were, here I was a kid from a small town in West Virginia, apparently about to undertake a here-to-fore undreamt of task. My mind was very active that afternoon wondering just what I was supposed to do with elephants. I hadn't noticed any teak forests in Georgia, and I certainly didn't think I could wrestle them into submission. At any rate, our first meeting, "the elephants" and me, was not very encouraging.

So there we were, me standing there gawking, and this giant animal, who did not appear to have a friendly inch on her many-inched body. I figured the best thing to do was to let her get used to my looks and scent first, that's what you do with a dog…right? So for about the next week we alternated walking around staring at each other with just standing in one spot and staring at each other. After the first dozen or so charges Moja made at the gate, I figured the gate was going to hold her, so I didn't run nearly as far away on those later charges as I had on the first ones.

On about the eighth day I got up enough nerve to offer Moja a piece of fruit right out of my hand. I had been feeding her but it had been from long distance. Moja took the fruit with her trunk, stuffed it into her mouth and proceeded in giving me my first boxing lesson. As soon as the fruit disappeared into her mouth, she balled up the end of her trunk and sent it flying in the direction of my head.

Fortunately my nerves were sufficiently on edge to automatically send my body flying backwards about six feet. My body reacted quite well, however, my feet were still somewhat trusting and, consequently, they did not react with the same alacrity. This automatic reaction saved my favorite head but did little for my posterior, which impacted the entrance road with a great deal of force. Bruised butt not withstanding, I found it a satisfactory trade-off.

It was at this point that I decided that I had to find a way to punish this animal somehow, or I wouldn't make it to twenty-two years of age (some people may flinch at this punishment stuff, but bear with me, it was survival time, remember). How do you punish an animal that was a foot and a half taller than you and has you outweighed by about twenty-five times. After a great deal of deliberation I hit on the idea of a switch. Yes, a switch, just like the one your dad used to tell you to go out and get so that he could beat you with it.

Anyway, I figured the elephant might be surprised at being attacked by a piece of food. You see elephants eat bushes and things. I found out later that elephants will frequently pick up sticks and beat themselves about the head and legs for fun. The youngsters love to do this, I figure their parents tell them to go out and get a switch to beat them with, and the youngsters are simply trying to reduce the potential effect.

Anyway, I had to try something. So, for about a week, every time Moja charged the gate, I would run up, yelling and screaming, smack her with the stick, and run like heck. To this day I will never really understand why this tactic worked, but it did. It may be that Moja was so shocked by this strange creature (me), and its behavior, that she just wanted to find out what was going to happen in the long run. (I used a stick for my entire career. I would sometimes use an elephant hook for show, but I always preferred a stick, much to the chagrin of all the "real" elephant men I met.)

Just about the time Moja stopped charging me, here comes Bill York back to see me. At this stage of the game I didn't need any more problems. Bill walks up and looks around and says "How's everything Frank?" I mutter something about not being dead *yet*. Bill then says "Good, you can get into the barn with her any time you want to." Bill then turns, gets into his jeep and drives away. I was really beginning to dislike Bill York's humor. My biggest concern, however, was that Bill might not have a sense of humor.

It turned out that that same day was one of the turning points in my career as an animal man. I said to myself "I came into this thing with no preconceived notions, I've got to give it my best shot." At that, I turned and walked toward the barn, picked up my switch (you have heard of security blankets, this is the first security switch), climbed over the gate, and found myself standing inside the elephant barn, face to face with 4000 pounds of BEAST. When I was inside the barn, I had the impression that this creature was three times as big as she had been when I was outside the barn (funny how sizes change dramatically, like your childhood things appear much smaller once you have grown). I think Moja must have been as shocked as I was, because from that day on, she was never aggressive towards me again.

Moja and I got along great after that. I fed her and cared for her and we grew very close. I had noticed that from time to time Moja would scream as if she were in great pain and grab at her back legs with her trunk. During these episodes she would slam into the walls with her tusks. I knew she had been doing this sort of thing for quite some time because her tusks were worn down flat, right next to where they came out of her gum line. I asked about her past and found out that she had been kept in a small concrete pen at the zoo she came from. She had been in that place for so long that the zoo had to knock the door frame off just to get her out. Considering this, I figured she must have some kind of arthritic condition which was giving her the pain.

When Bill York finally gave me the go-ahead to take Moja out of the elephant barn, I was scared to death. However, I knew that I had to get her out and exercise her to back to good health. For about the first week I just took her out around the barn itself. She really seemed to enjoy even this little bit of freedom. Her attitude really improved remarkably.

Since the park wasn't open yet, I sort of had the run of the whole hoof stock area. I gradually increased the distance and duration of our walks until we finally reached an area where a spring ran down and filled up a small gully near the road. After it rained, the water would be fairly deep and very muddy (with that famous Georgia red clay). Our usual itinerary was to walk around a while until it warmed up and then I would take moja to this "pond."

Elephants love water, and Moja was no exception. It wasn't long before she really looked forward to lying in the mud during our walks. She would wade into the water, blow it all over her, then go down on her belly in the mud and just lie there for up to a half hour at a time. I knew that getting her weight off her joints would be good for her, and the cool water seemed to ease her pain.

For about two weeks there didn't seem to be a significant change in her condition; she walked as if she were walking on eggshells (she didn't limp noticeably—it is very difficult to limp on all your legs at the same time). After this time I did begin to notice that her episodes of pain were coming further and further apart. Finally, about three months later, she stopped having the pain episodes completely. I never noticed another episode after that. After that Moja started putting on weight and began to look and act like a real elephant.

Helping Moja was one of the most satisfying things I have ever done, knowing that my actions had relieved some suffering from an animal who had been mistreated. Not only did Moja regain her health but she seemed to gain a trust in me which resulted in my "adoption" by her. We grew very close. Moja took it upon herself to become my protector. You can imagine what it might be like to have an elephant as a body guard.

One example of Moja's new role as body guard came about one day as I was taking the elephants (at the time of this incident I had twelve of them) to the big lake for a swim. I suppose most people have heard of the reputation of the African cape buffalo. We had five cape buffalo at the park, two males and three females. The big bull was not very friendly (sort of an understatement for cape buffalo, I know, but I'm trying to be nice).

We had built a road on top of the dam that was constructed to create our large lake. This dam was just wide enough for the two-lane roadway on top of it. One side of the dam dropped off dramatically and was bordered by a ten foot tall chain link fence. The other side of the dam was the water from the lake created by the dam. The elephants and I had just about gotten all the way across the dam when I noticed the cape buffalo standing at the top of the hill above the causeway.

If it had just been *me* noticing *them* it would have been alright, but *they* noticed *me* too. As I slowly turned around to try to ease my way back across the causeway, the cape buffalo charged. I had doubts about outrunning a charging cape buffalo, but these doubts were rapidly replaced by an attempt at decision making. Was I to attempt to climb the fence or just jump into the lake.

I took off running as fast as I could back across the causeway, scattering elephants as I went. The elephants soon caught on, and passed me screaming and crying. After the elephants had left me in the dust, there was nothing between me and the charging buffalo. Moja seemed to realize this at the same time I did. She stopped, turned around, (for just an instant I thought she was going to run over me for getting her into this predicament, but I had misjudged her), ran past me, and charged at the charging cape buffalo, ears out and screaming to wake the dead.

If you have ever seen the charge of an upset elephant you'll realize why what happened next happened. If you can imagine a cape buffalo having a first thought (let alone a second one) these cape buffalo did. They stopped, turned around, and ran away just as fast as their legs could carry them. It was about the time that the buffalo turned that Moja turned back around and ran back past me and off the causeway. I tell you, it was an emotional group which got together to "discuss" our close encounter of the worst kind. From that moment on, I realized I had no need to fear while Moja was with me, and I never loved her more.

There was another instance when Moja's body guard duties came into play. This time it wasn't an animal but another employee of the park. I was down watching the elephants when this new employee pulls up. I had never met him before, and when he got out of the jeep I wondered how he had gotten into the jeep. He must have been six foot six and two hundred and fifty pounds. He starts telling me about how he is going to go down to the elephant barn and take my tools because he needs them. I might have been a foot shorter and seventy pounds lighter but I was still a pretty feisty guy (You kinda gotta be a feisty guy to be an elephant man, don't ya see).

During the ensuing argument, I completely forgot about the elephants. Just about the time that this guy is going to start pounding me into the ground, a giant head appears right over my shoulder, imposing itself between this guy and me. Yep, Moja had come over to see what was up. She had a look in her eye that I knew meant trouble. This guy looked at me, and looked at Moja and (I must say this in his behalf, he was very perceptive) got her message quite clearly. He turned around, hopped (an interesting act for one his size) into the jeep and drove off. I can't remember ever seeing him around the elephant section after that.

Well, I grabbed Moja around the neck and gave her a big hug. She seemed to say "you're welcome" and just went back to whatever she was doing. It was times like these that made me wonder what fool ever coined the phrase "dumb animals." Obviously he had never been as close to any of them as I have.

Although Moja was my first elephant she was by no means my last. And even though I hold a special place in my heart for all of them, I will undoubtably always love Moja best. After Lion Country closed, they sent Moja to the Knoxville Zoo in Tennessee where she was well treated. The Knoxville zoo was the first zoo in the country in recent times to raise African elephants.

About ten years after she was moved, I went to the Knoxville zoo to see her. She looked good. I called her name and she stopped what she was doing, a half eaten piece of hay hanging out of her mouth. She raised her head and looked around as if the voice had been in her head. Elephants don't have superior vision so she could not have recognized me by sight. She got this look on her face as if to say "Nah, couldn't be," and went on with her eating. I didn't press the issue. She was apparently happy, healthy, and satisfied with her lot. I left the zoo that day wondering if she remembered me, and if so, if her memories of me were as found as my memories of her.

# Chapter 2: Amos

We had discussed the trip to Omaha that weekend. All the plans were made for my leaving Monday morning, early. We had figured it was about 1000 miles to Omaha from Atlanta, so, at an average of fifty miles per hour, I should arrive there very early Tuesday morning. I would sack out for a couple of hours in the truck, and roll into the zoo when it opened. I would arrive at the Henry Doorly Zoo, where everything was supposed to be ready to go, pick up my load, and head back for Atlanta right away. We figured I should be back by Wednesday afternoon.

Oh, by the way, I was going to Omaha to pick up two young lions, and a three ton bull African elephant by the name of Amos. My vehicle for the trip was a Dodge Powerwagon 200 pickup truck, pulling an eighteen foot lowboy trailer. To be attached to the trailer was a rhinoceros crate, "modified" to carry the elephant.

Monday morning rolled around and the work to convert the rhino crate into an elephant crate was not complete. These rhino crates are built in Africa (not surprisingly, that is where we get our white rhinos from) out of two-inch thick, very hard wood, with angle iron reinforcements on the outside. The crates are hand made and, consequently, vary in size. This one was about ten feet long and five feet wide. Originally it had been about six feet tall.

The front and back of these crates are hinged so that they can be opened. Just inside the doors of the Rhino crates are several three inch wide galvanized pipes, which run from holes in the top of the crate through holes in the bottom of the crates. These pipes are bolted to the angle iron at the top of the crate. We took the pipes out of the front and back of this particular crate for this trip, leaving just the massive doors. We felt they would be sufficient to hold this elephant in.

Modifications to the crate involved cutting the angle iron at the top of the crate, adding additional height to the crate, (rhinos are considerable shorter than elephants) so that it could accommodate the seven to eight foot tall elephant, then welding the top back on. The spaces created by this modification, in the front, back, and sides of the crate, were filled by bolting three-quarter inch plywood over the angle iron. This plywood was inside the external braces on the sides of the crate, but the front and back pieces of plywood had no external support. A factor which resulted in some additional modifications on the trip back.

We worked all day getting the crate ready and attaching it, by means of chains and load-binders, to the lowboy. A load-binder is a long handle with two hooks on it. When the hooks are attached, one to the chain, and one to the truck bed, upon closing the handle, the chain is pulled tight and can be secured. A lowboy is simply a flat trailer which is built very low to the ground. The wheels are on the side, rather than under the trailer. It is important to keep the weight of your load as low as possible, so that you have greater stability. With an elephant standing up, and rocking back and forth, you need to reduce the strain on the system as much as possible.

After the crate was attached, I had to make sure my travel papers were in order. I failed to mention before, that this was my first solo animal hauling experience. I'd been in the animal business all of two months.

At about five thirty in the afternoon, I was finally ready to go. I boarded the truck and I was off. Having never done anything like this before, and hauling a very top-heavy trailer, my expected fifty mile per hour average turned out to be closer to thirty miles per hour.

I pulled into the outskirts of Omaha around midnight Tuesday night. I stopped at a rest area, and went to sleep in the cab of the truck. I set my alarm for seven, and when it went off, I felt as if I had just that minute fallen asleep. Nevertheless, I woke myself up and headed into Omaha. I had to stop and ask directions to the zoo two or three times, but I finally made it. When I got there, there was a chain hanging between two posts blocking off the service road to the zoo. I parked the truck and walked into the zoo, to find out what my next move was going to be.

I stopped this fellow who was walking by, and together we rounded up somebody who was expecting me (it was a relief that they did, in fact, know I was coming). He said the first thing we should load was the elephant, so I walked back to the truck, and backed the truck and trailer down this ramp into the bottom of their elephant barn. Their elephants were housed underground, below their display area. This fellow said all we had to do was run the elephant into the crate. It took us about an hour to secure the area around the truck, and build a ramp for Amos, the elephant. I found out they were selling him because their two older elephants sort of beat him up, occasionally.

After about four hours of trying to run Amos into the crate, we all decided to develop an alternative plan. The zoo employees decided to try to slowly work Amos up to the crate by closing off more and more of his escape route with a jeep moving slowly in from behind. The sides of his escape route were blocked with the big steel gates from the elephant barn itself. After having gotten him up near the trailer and crate, they sent for a tractor and some rope.

They backed the tractor down in front of my truck. Next, they attached this huge rope to the back of this tractor, over the top of my truck, and into the front of the crate. They then pulled the rope through the crate and out the back. Then they proceeded to tie the rope around Amos' left front leg. As the tractor slowly took up the slack from the front, everyone jumped in to help push this big elephant from the back. Some how or another, we got Amos into the crate.

We didn't just get him into the crate, we wedged him in. You see, Amos was a good healthy big elephant. This elephant just barely fit into the crate. Oh the crate was apparently tall enough (we will talk about this in a few minutes) but it was quite narrow. We secured the back doors, got the rope off Amos' foot and went to pick up the lions.

Getting the lions into their crate was easy. However, we then had to pick the crate up and load it into the back of the pick-up, in front of the lowboy, with Amos in the crate on the lowboy. You must realize that the lion crate was made of plywood, and had lots of holes drilled in it for air for the lions. Unfortunately, these holes were big enough for fingers to slip into, or claws and fangs to come out of.

Even with some boards nailed unto the sides of the crate for hand holds, it was still a comedy of errors trying to get that crate into the back of the pick-up. Every so often one or another of us would suddenly let go of his part of the crate due to the fear of losing a finger or two. The lions apparently did not like being in the crate, and, consequently, were taking their frustrations out on us. They were moving around and trying to grab us through those air holes. Nobody got too badly injured, one or two of us did get strained muscles when someone suddenly let go of their part of the crate. However, we finally did get the crate in the truck.

I was all ready to head for home when, upon checking on Amos for the last time, I found he had apparently slipped down, and was wedged in the bottom of the crate, on his chest. This wouldn't normally be a problem, except that an elephant has to sort of throw his front knee out from under his body in order for him to stand up, and the crate was just too small for Amos to do that. Besides, elephants use a little different system of breathing compared with other animals means of breathing. They rely almost solely on their intercostal muscles (rib muscles), rather than their diaphragm. They cannot spend too much time on their chest, because their breathing capability is reduced and they could suffocate.

The zoo staff and I conferred for a few minutes and decided to try to get him up while he was still in the crate. I drove out to a parking lot on the zoo grounds (I think they wanted to make certain that if we got Amos up on his feet, that they could send me on my way quickly, so they wouldn't have to worry about him slipping down again.). Together with the veterinarian, the handlers and I started working to get Amos on his feet again.

We got that same rope that we used to help pull Amos into the truck and (with a great deal of difficulty) the vet finally got the rope around Amos' butt. We then ran the rope up through the top of the crate, and fastened it unto a jeep. However, try as it might, that little Jeep just couldn't raise that big old butt off the floor of the crate. Finally, we tied the loose end of the rope to a big old oak tree. I got into the truck (remember, those Dodge Powerwagons were powerhouses), put the truck into low four-wheel drive, and very slowly, guided by the vet, drove forward. For a few minutes we thought we were going to fail again, but just then, Amos figured out what we were doing, and decided to help us help him stand up.

Finally, with one last check of my hail and hardy cargo, it was back on the road. It was about six o'clock Wednesday evening by that time. I don't think the staff at the Henry Doorly Zoo was ever as happy to see anybody leave their zoo than they were when I pulled out of their parking lot that evening.

Amos soon got the message that he wasn't being watched so carefully, and started to redesign his specially redesigned crate. The first thing to go was the piece of plywood covering the front area of the extended crate. This piece of plywood had simply been nailed to the plywood that had been added to the sides. As I looked into my rear view mirror, I saw this piece of plywood swing out over the oncoming traffic (I was still on the residential roads which surround the zoo), as if the left side of it were on hinges. I stopped the truck, right in the road, (fortunately there wasn't much traffic) and got out of the truck, to do—I didn't know what. About the time I was about to try to figure out what to do, Amos solved that problem for me. He reached up an knocked that piece of plywood the rest of the way off.

I simply bent down, picked up that piece of plywood, and threw it unto the lowboy. I then hopped back into the cab of the truck, and steeled myself to watching that huge trunk stick through the front of that crate and "test the wind" from time to time. As I have said, I was forced to go through some residential streets to get back unto the interstate. Most of these streets had big old trees growing right next to the road, with branches hanging low over the street.

I had stopped at a stop light on just such a street, when I noticed the car coming the other direction pointing and looking at my truck. I looked in my mirror and here was this trunk coming out of the front of the crate, casually breaking branches off this low hanging maple tree, and stuffing them into the crate. Well, he was only doing what came naturally. After the initial shock from some cars' occupants, most people seemed to get a kick out of it. However, one car did drive up into someone's yard while watching this show. I don't think there were too many tire tracks in too many peoples' yards. At any rate, I was kind of glad Amos had gotten his little "window to the world."

The trip back was fairly uneventful except at the truck weighing stations. I would pull up to the scales and each one of the operators would call me in to check my manifests. It seemed as though my weight wasn't corresponding to my size. I would take my papers in and get *the* question "What are you hauling, horses?" I would then give them *the* answer "No sir, and elephant." I would generally be delayed for just enough time for everyone to get a good look at Amos. I didn't worry about anyone getting too close to the elephant crate. If I saw they were getting too close, I would tell them there were two lions in the bed of the pick-up. After that, I'd usually be sent on my way.

Around about the middle of Tennessee I was really getting tired, remember, this was Thursday night, and I had been going since Monday morning with only seven hours of sleep Tuesday night. I even decided to pull over once or twice to shake the cobwebs out of my brain. I forgot to tell you that, with the way the truck and trailer were set up, as long as Amos stayed up near the front of the crate, the weight distribution was satisfactory, and the truck and trailer rode fairly well. However, when Amos rocked back to the back of the crate, it put altogether too much weight on the back end of the trailer, the truck would slow down significantly, and would weave from side to side. I could only go at most twenty-five miles an hour when Amos rocked back, and that didn't improve my mood much.

What with my exhaustion, and Amos's antics, I pulled into a truck stop just north of Atlanta at about ten in the morning on Friday. I figured I was home free, it was daylight out, and I had caught my third or forth wind. I estimated I had a little more that two hours left to go and, since I was a day and a half late already, I probably could afford to spend a little time and get myself a good breakfast.

I had a lot of coffee, and some breakfast, and I felt a lot better. I felt better, that is until I checked on my cargo. Amos was lying down again. I was in a panic, better than two hours left to go on the trip and Amos was down. I rushed back to the café and called the park and told them the whole situation. They said they would alert the police, and ask them not to stop me. They told me to get in the truck, head it for home, and keep the gas pedal on the floor. They said they would be ready to unload as soon as I pulled in.

I got back on the road and kept my foot to the floor. I would be able to go faster without Amos moving around in the crate. There was a time or two when I believe I had a police escort, but I was too focused on my driving to really be sure. I rolled in through the open park gates at about noon Friday. I backed down into the elephant barn area at the park, where they had this big crane standing by. They detached the crate from the lowboy, picked it up with the crane, and set it down in the doorway of the elephant barn.

The barn had two sides. The left side of the barn, as you faced it, housed several small elephants which had come in while I was away. On the right side was Moja. Amos and Moja would live together for a while. We opened the door of the crate and the barn gate, and Amos sort of rolled out of the crate. He was a little befuddled, but apparently none the worse for the wear.

The welcome Amos got was about the same sort of thing he had had for the last three days. As soon as he rolled into the pen, Moja gave him a punch to the head. Amos struggled to his feet, Moja saw how big he was, and left him alone after that. The first meeting notwithstanding, Amos and Moja soon became good friends.

My boss looked at me and asked me just how much sleep I had gotten since Monday morning. I told him about ten hours all together. He sent me home for a couple of days. I guess I was the one in the worst shape of all of us who participated in that trip.

That was my first animal hauling adventure and my first meeting with Amos. Over the next two years I developed a close friendship with Amos but when I left Lion Country I lost track of him. I haven't seen Amos since 1976.

While I have you thinking about the animal hauling business, let me tell you a story about one other trip I took. Not all of the exciting times occurred at the places I worked. There were other times when I was involved in someone else's "fun." One hot summer day, I was making a pickup at a medium sized southern zoo, when the animal people told me they needed a hand to move a polar bear. The polar bear is the largest land carnivore. I had never handled a polar bear, so was quite excited about the opportunity.

The zoo was rearranging its exhibits, and was moving some of their animals from display to display. They had most of the animals moved, but still had a large male polar bear to move. This bear was huge, well over 1200 pounds. The plan was to dart the bear in his display area, then carry him through the service area behind the exhibits to his new area. That is why they asked me to help, they needed all the bodies they could get to carry 1200 pounds of tranquilized polar bear.

The exhibit area was constructed of gunnite. Gunnite is concrete, sprayed on a wire form, which simulates rock. Behind the exhibit was a narrow enclosed service area from which the animals could be fed. Access to the exhibits was through small steel doors which opened into the service area. The service area was about eight feet wide.

After their veterinarian darted the bear, we waited for the allotted time to make certain that the bear was under the influence of the drug. After some brave soul was the first to poke the bear's prostrate form, to see if he was completely under the influence of the immobilization drug, we all filed into the exhibit and got around the bear. This thing was enormous. It had lots of loose skin, and so we had hand holds all the way around. Those individuals who got a foot, soon saw that each foot was larger than their own heads. The head of this massive bear was more than enough for two people to carry, and contained the biggest canine teeth I had ever seen, nearly three inches long.

We dragged and struggled this big bear through the small door behind the display, and into the rear service area. There were about twelve of us, and this bear, wedged into this service area only eight feet wide. We were constantly stumbling and letting go of our holds, as we would bang into the sides of the corridor or each other, or loose our grips. First the weight of the bear would swing towards one side, then it would swing towards the other side. On occasion, someone would get pinned against the wall by the sheer weight of this beast.

As we were struggling down the hallway, looking like a group of giant ants with a choice bit of food, the bear woke up. Now, this wasn't supposed to happen. We were not prepared for this event. The drug the vet used was supposed to keep this bear out for plenty long enough for us to get him moved. Oh well, you know what they say about the "best laid schemes of mice and men."

Despite all of the logic which said this bear would not wake up, he woke up anyway (Sometimes animals can be so hard-headed, (see George). I guess we should have let the bear read the script.). At the moment he awoke, everyone in that small area became profoundly aware of their surroundings. Here we were, twelve people, jammed into a narrow hallway, with twelve hundred pounds of polar bear who probably wasn't in a very good mood.

If you have ever seen film of rats leaving a sinking ship, or cartoon characters trying to escape some imminent peril, you have seen them climb all over each other in their attempt to escape. Well folks, that is the scene which took place in that corridor behind the bear exhibit that day. If you were just a little bit slow, someone climbed over you to get out of the way. It was like a scene out of some horror movie, every man for himself.

I can't remember exactly what happened after that. I looked around, and I was standing on the grass in back of the exhibit building. As I looked around, I saw two or three people holding their chests, and breathing hard. I didn't know where everyone else was. I know we all got to some kind of shelter, some people pushing each other out of the rear doors, and some people running the entire length of the service area (They may still be at the end of that corridor, waiting for the "all clear").

I know that the bear had awakened and gotten to his feet, but apparently had enough drug in him to prevent him from doing much else, thank goodness. I do know that it was some time before a new plan was conceived and executed. This plan succeeded in coercing the bear into his new home. After this excitement, I was glad to get my truck loaded up and head on down the road to a somewhat more controlled chaos.

# Chapter 3: Lion Country Punks

Let me tell you a bit about the little elephants I mentioned in the last chapter, the ones who were waiting for me in the barn when I got back with Amos. They were five young African elephants ranging in age from one and one-half to three years old. There was one male and four females. Working with these elephants was an entirely different matter than working with Moja. Although they didn't intimidate me as much as Moja did, the biggest still weighed nearly 1000 pounds. For a long time I simply fed them, cleaned up after them (another story all together), and watched them.

By observing them, I learned how they expressed dominance and submission. I figured instead of teaching them a whole new set of rules and a whole new language (the rules and language of *Homo sapiens*...us), I would just adopt the rules and language they instinctively knew. After all, I was supposed to possess the superior intellect. It was a very gallant idea which, in the long run turned out for the best, but, at the time, didn't prepare me for just how painful it would be to put into practice.

After watching the punks (that is what us elephant men call little elephants) for some time, and learning their pecking order, I decided it was time for me to become their leader. I had gotten to know each one's personality pretty well, and they had become familiar with me. (I have found it to be true that the young of most species adapt much more quickly than the adults, who seem to be quite set in their ways.)

I started my climb to elephant supremacy from the bottom. I went into the pen, walked up to my chosen animal, and did the elephant counterpart of tossing down the gauntlet. This amounts to giving your challenger a punch in the side. For elephants, they give each other a good shot with the front of their faces (trunk rolled up under their chin out of the way). This is easier for them than it would have been for me, so I settled for just punching the side of my chosen punk. (Considering the texture of an elephant's hide, this practice is not recommended for those wishing to keep skin on their knuckles)

The elephant turned "on his heels" (It is amazing how some very large, and very heavy animals can make this maneuver, including elephants, rhinos, and hippopotamuses.), and promptly accepted my challenge. Her response left me on my backside, on the floor, and forced me to leave the pen to recuperate and reevaluate my plan of attack. I realized that the gentlemanly method did not work, so I decided to try a somewhat more forceful approach. I have found out, since that time, that loud noise and a show of aggression, are the major components of most animal dominance battles. Armed with my new battle plan, I jumped into the pen, yelling at the top of my lungs, and ran into my chosen elephant, sideways. To my surprise, she turned her backside to me, signifying that I had won the contest. You don't know how happy I was to have finally figured these critters out. Little did I know that there would be many more battles before the war was over.

I left the pen. I then began to plan my move up the ranks, by challenging the next highest elephant on the totem pole. By the way, the other elephants seemed to be wondering just what the devil was going on, here was this two-legged creature, screaming, and running around like a maniac. But, as I said, young animals get used to things much more easily than older animals, and it wasn't long before the elephants were used to my bizarre behavior. There was one other problem associated with this sort of behavior, however. It seemed that my supervisors at work never did understand just what I was doing. Fortunately, I was getting results, and that was all that was required of me, for the time being.

Anyway, when I went into the pen to perform my attack on the second lowest ranking individual, the elephants were kind of edgy. I let out a yell and ran headlong into the side of my target elephant. It appeared to have the desired effect. As I paused to gloat over my success, I was hit hard in the side, and knocked against the wall. I turned around and there was the elephant I thought had been my first conquest standing with what looked to all the world like a big grin on her face. My new tactic appeared to have had the desired affect, but I added a new twist, to make sure the elephants knew it was one at a time. After my charge, and the appropriate response from the given animal, I would run like heck for safe ground.

I now had seven African elephants, two fairly good size ones, and five smaller ones. Bill said I could name them, so I got a Swahili dictionary from him, and sat down to study the personalities of my new charges, and see if I could name them appropriately. After some searching, I decided that their new names would be Umfan, Shalati, Chidsa, Kiasi, and Urena.

Umfan was my favorite. He was absolutely round. He weighed about 1000 pounds when I got him, and he even had these big fat cheeks. He was comfortable with me from the beginning. We would hang around together, and play. He is the only elephant that would give me his trunk, and then let it go completely limp. I could even tie it in a knot, and he would just stand there and bob his head like it was the greatest fun. Umfan also took a shine to Amos. When Amos would tolerate it, Umfan would suck on the bottom of Amos' ear like he was sucking on a pacifier. Umfan would do that whenever he could, and for long periods of time. Umfan was the most dominant of the original five punks.

Shalati was the third dominant of the first group of punks. She weighed about 900 pounds. She was the smartest elephant I ever had. She was very receptive to training, but was smart enough to get out of it if she wanted to. She was a beautiful little elephant, very "feminine" looking with long eyelashes. People were frequently surprised that I could tell little elephants apart. However, after you work with animals for a while, they get to look as different as people do.

Shalati's favorite trick occurred during our walks around the hoofstock section. She would always be out in the front of the herd when we moved. She would find the feeding stations for the hoof stock, and grab a couple of trunksful of sweetfeed before I could get up there and chase her away. She would run off, sweetfeed spilling all over the place, as she tried to stuff as much of what she had grabbed with her trunk into her mouth. As she was leaving one feeder, she was on the lookout for the next one down the road. We played that game of "first to the feeder" a lot.

Chidsa was a punk of about 1000 pounds who, it turned out, had a misalignment of her molars, and consequently, was not chewing up her food adequately. She would get impacted from eating roots out in the hoof stock section, and I would have to treat her until she passed the bolus. This treatment involved getting her to drink mineral oil. I tried a lot of ways to try to get her to drink it.

Remember, elephants pull the liquid they are drinking up into their trunks and squirt it into their mouths. This process allows them to smell and feel the stuff they are drinking before they drink it. I finally discovered that Chidsa loved Gatoraide. I would pour the mineral oil in the Gatoraide in a big rubber tub (the oil would float on the top, of course). Then I would have splash my hand back and forth to mix the two liquids while she drank her "medicine." We sold her in the fall of 1972 to a zoo who could guarantee that she would only get food that was chopped up before she got it.

Kiasi was small, about 800 pounds, and peaceful little elephant with a very thin pointed face. She was never any trouble and always kept a low profile.

Urena was a small round elephant, about 800 pounds, who was very strong willed. She was the only one of the punks who would play-fight with Umfan. Most of the other punks would not stand to get pushed around by the fat one. She was very difficult to control on occasion, but never caused any trouble.

I got the next group of elephants in about three months. Seven elephants came in, but I only got to keep six females. I named them Sabi, Sikivu, Nafsi, Uhuru, Hisani, Saburi, and Sauti.

Sabi was one of the elephants which came in with the seven, but he was way too little to live in the elephant barn, so we put him in a special enclosure in the entertainment area called Cuddle Corner. Sabi was a little male elephant with lots of hair all over his body. He was the cutest, nicest little elephant and only weighed a few hundred pounds. The girls who worked in the Cuddle Corner just loved Sabi.

Sikivu was a 1000 pound female who was very easy going. She always seemed to just "go along with the crowd." She fit in easily with the other punks, Amos, and Moja.

Nafsi was a nut. She was very high strung and nervous. If anyone, or anything, said "Boo" to her, she was off like a shot. She was stocky, and was one of the larger punks at 1100 pounds, but she could outrun me and all of the other elephants put together. I can remember, just after I got her, she would take off and I would take off after her. After running myself breathless several times, however, I eventually just let her run. You see she was so nervous that she couldn't be out in the hoofstock section too long before she got scared and came running back to the security of the other elephants.

Uhuru was the biggest of the punks. at 1200 pounds, she only outweighed Nafsi by 100 pounds, but as Nafsi was stocky, Uhuru was lanky. She had a thin, narrow body, and long thin legs. Uhuru means peace in Swahili, and that is one thing that Uhuru and I never had between us. She was smart, hard headed, and big.

She never really did accept me as the boss, but she took second place to Umfan right away, and Umfan and I were best buddies. She was always watching me out of the corner of her eye, to see what I was up to. She was never a threat to me, except when we were in the barn. Then she would sometimes take a swing at me if she thought she could get away with it.

Hisani was the cutest little bundle of insecurity. She wanted desperately to have the relationship Umfan had with me, but she never could quite get the wildness out of herself. She would elicit attention, then, when I turned to give it to her, she would bolt a few feet, shake her head and snort. You could see the conflict going on in her mind. She never did calm down all the way, but she was a good elephant and never gave me any trouble. When I moved to my next job, I arranged to buy Kiasi, and stayed with her for about four years all together.

Saburi was a nice little elephant that had some trouble off and on with stiffness in her hind legs. I would have to keep her up in the barn from time to time to treat her, and make sure she was OK. Finally we moved her up to the entertainment area and put her in with Sabi. She was considerably bigger than he was, at 1000 pounds, but they got along quite well, and Sabi liked the company.

Sauti was a nice little elephant who weighed about 1000 pounds. She seemed fairly weak when she arrived, and had to be treated for a severe infection in her forehead soon after she got to lion country. This infection lingered for a couple of months, with the vet doing everything he could to treat it. I remember giving her lots of shots when the elephants were in the barn. We moved her up to the cuddle corner area for a couple of weeks with Sabi and Saburi, but we soon had to confine her to an enclosed hut. We moved Saburi into the hut with her to keep her company. She was in the hut under constant medication for another couple of weeks.

I found her "down" on the morning of the twentieth of November. When an animal is "down", that means that they are so sick that they can't even get up on their feet. I stayed with the two elephants round the clock after that morning. From time to time I would give Sauti intravenous fluids in one of the veins in the back of her ear. During the times when she did stand up, I would have to walk around following her, holding the bottle up so that the fluids could continue. At eleven o'clock on the night of November 22 Sauti died.

I removed her body from the hut in which the two elephants had been held, because Saburi was extremely upset. After removing her body from the hut, I went back into the hut to stay with Saburi for the night. I had been awake since the morning of the twentieth, so I was very tired. I laid down on a pile of hay in the hut, not even thinking about Saburi being there and what she might do if I was asleep. I was convinced that that was my last day in the animal business anyway, because the pain of losing that little elephant was so great. I decided I would quit the next morning when my boss got to work.

At about daybreak I awoke. I was still very tired, and somewhat disoriented. As my senses awoke, I remembered what had happened, and that I was lying on a bed of hay in a hut. I had my right arm out perpendicular to my body. Lying, sound asleep, with her back to me and her head ever so carefully over my arm, was Saburi. It brings back the tears of joy I shed that morning, just to write these words. I decided not to leave the animal business. You see, the animals needed me. I learned that you must do the very best you can do, but if you still fail, life must go on. There were lots of other individuals depending on me.

During the day, I would take the elephants out of the elephant barn. After I started to take the elephants out of the barn and walk them around the hoof stock section, I needed to have some way to carry treats for them, so that I could reward them if they did something I wanted them to do. This is the easiest way to train an animal. Wait till they do something you like, then give them some kind of positive reinforcement. I did this with my dog, and she is as "smart" and well trained as those dogs in the movies.

Anyway, I needed something that I didn't have to carry, but had lots of storage space. I discovered that those big army fatigue coats, with the four big pockets, worked out just fine. I would fill up my pockets in the morning with things like Monkey Chow (Monkey Chow is biscuits, specially designed for primates, made by Purina. Yes, Purina makes "Chow" for just about anything, not just Dog Chow.) If I could keep the elephants from reaching into my pockets and stealing all of the Monkey Chow first thing in the morning, I could get it to last for several hours.

One day, early on in my life as the elephant man at Lion Country, Bill York told me that they had to come down and close up the barn, so that it would be warm enough for the winter. The barn had been constructed very quickly because the elephants were arriving and, consequently, had not been completely finished. The additional construction included laying new block for the walls, and painting the outside. Everyone wondered how they would keep the new construction intact, with a bunch of elephants messing with it all night.

I said that I would keep the elephants out all night and watch them, if they could get the construction done in the two days. Everyone seemed skeptical about this offer, but I was persuasive, and they finally let me try it. I remember the thoughts which ran through my head as the sun slowly set and twilight overtook us. I was wondering how I was going to control a bunch of elephants I couldn't even see. There were no lights down at the elephant barn area.

The elephants were nervous as dark fell. They were used to being put up in their nice safe barn at night. They kept wanting to go back to the barn, and I had to chase them away from the new construction. For those of you who think that elephants don't want to go into their barns at night, let me ease your concern. I had the devil of a time keeping them out of the barn when the end of the day came. It was difficult to keep them on display. They wanted to go home and rest. On any given day, if they got past me, they would go down and stand inside the barn for hours, with the gates wide open.

As the elephants settled down, I sat down on the cinder block wall near the barn. I had left the elephants out in a large, heavily treed holding area near the elephant barn. As night drew on, I could see the large silhouettes of the elephants, moving slowly in the trees off to my right. I must have dozed off around about midnight because, when I looked again for the elephants, I couldn't make out any shapes in the gloom.

I bolted wide awake and hopped off the wall to go look for my elephants. My thoughts were prayers. Prayers that, first, I would find them, second, they would all be together, and third, that they would still be in Georgia somewhere. My fears were allayed when, upon walking up to the little ridge where they had been, I found myself surrounded by elephants. Oh, these elephants weren't behaving quite like any I had ever seen before, but they were at least here.

You see, the elephants, all of them, were lying flat out on their sides on the ground, snoring away. They were all fast asleep, and did not even wake up when I walked in among them. I eased myself back down to the barn, said a prayer of thanks, and proceeded to try to keep myself awake for the rest of the night. This wasn't easy, since I had to sit there and listen to the peaceful snores of the sleeping elephants who were getting a good night's rest. On many occasions I have been told that elephants, or horses, or giraffes, don't lie down to sleep. I can tell you from personal experience, they do so!

# Chapter 4: A Little More About Me

This is a book about animal stories, but I thought I would tell you about how I got into the animal business in the first place. I was born and raised in the town of Fairmont, West Virginia. I had an interesting childhood (there is another book altogether). My father was a very popular obstetrician in town. Everybody knew Doc Evans. We had enough money when I was growing up so that I grew up rather spoiled. As a result of this, I never really did study in high school, and when I got to college, I didn't bother to go to class. This tendency not to go to class resulted in my finally being removed from the university systems, and home I came to figure out just what it was that I would do with the rest of my life.

My parents went to Dallas, Texas to visit my sister during the time I was a twenty-one year old grocery store bag-boy, living at home, and bothering my parents. When they returned, they handed me a brochure. I can remember that moment to this day, I was about halfway up the stairs from the family room, and they had stopped at the top of the stairs in the kitchen. I stood on the stairs and read this brochure. The brochure said Lion Country Safari African Tours. It had beautiful color pictures of African animals and, upon opening it, I realized that this was an application to go on a tour of Africa. Not just any ordinary tour however, this tour was designed to incorporate the tranquilization and capture of the Southern White Rhinoceros.

I can still remember my parents just standing on the top step patiently watching me. I remember all the thoughts that flowed through my mind that morning, paramount among them was the one I expressed to my parents. I looked up at them and said "If you send me on this trip, you will never have to worry about what I am going to do with my life anymore." You see, it was my intention to use this opportunity to get into the animal business. I didn't know what I would do, or how I would accomplish my goal, I was just certain that this was the "break" I needed.

I had always been fascinated with animals, as a kid I had all the normal pets (except cats, but that's another story.) Along with the normal pets; dogs, hamsters, parakeets, fish, etc; I would also acquire some not so normal pets; like snakes, lizards, frogs, and when we went to Florida, caimans. For those of you who traveled in Florida back then, most of those "Live Baby Alligators" were caimans from South America. Anyway, back to my story. I watched all of those animal shows that were on TV in the sixties, and every time I would see Marlon Perkins tell Jim Fowler to go get this animal or that, I would say to myself "I can do that."

My parents did not have as much faith in this life-long decision-making thing as I did, but they did want me to experience this trip. So plans were made, the application was sent off, and in just a little while, I was packing to go to Africa. I remember, I had grown a moustache so I would look older, and as I boarded the plane, on a trip that would eventually change my life, I was wearing a new brown corduroy jacket. It was March, and cool in West Virginia. I was ready for Africa! Or so I thought, It was way too hot for corduroy.

There were thirteen of us on the tour, which was hosted by Lion Country Safari. We were met in New York by a fellow from the Lion Country Safari public relations department, who would accompany us on the trip. We flew from New York to Zurich and rested for an afternoon before boarding a plane which would take us from Zurich to Johannesburg, South Africa. The flight from Zurich to Johannesburg lasted ten hours, and was one of the most interesting flights I have ever taken.

The plane was crowded, and it felt as though I was in one of those buses you see in the South American adventure movies. The only thing missing was the livestock. People were eating strange things, and smoking strange things, all to the accompaniment of screaming babies and loud discussions in multiple languages. But the trip did have some major high points. It seems that on this trip the pilot flew using landmarks rather than following a map. This probably wasn't true, but it sure seemed like it. (Maybe it was true.)

After we crossed the Mediterranean, we followed the Nile river along its entire length. You could look out the window, if you could get to one, and see the famous Nile. I remember thinking about how much history was connected with that river. Thinking about the Pharaohs and their massive monuments to themselves. Of course the pyramids were not visible from where we were, but that led to an even greater ability to fantasize.

As we continued south, we eventually made it to Mount Kilimanjaro. So that everyone could see this most famous of African mountains, the pilot flew around it one way, then turned the plane around an flew around it the other way. It was pretty spectacular, and I was very impressed that the airline would do this sort of thing. Most of the time, as we flew, you could look down on vast plains dotted with little white cumulus clouds. That was Africa down there. The Africa we had seen all our lives in the Tarzan movies. Darkest Africa looked pretty bright and beautiful to me.

We had a fuel stop in Dar El Salaam, Tanzania. It turned out that the day we were flying by, they had a military coup in Tanzania. When we landed, refueling regulations forbade us from staying on the plane, so we were marched out to a waiting room in the top of the airplane terminal. Marched is the operative term here folks. There was a double line of soldiers, armed with automatic weapons, between the plane and the room. We were instructed not to do or say anything, but walk straight ahead and keep quiet. We did.

The room in which we were placed was not air conditioned. The room was just a bare room, where those of us from the plane sat, or stood, until the plane was refueled. After refueling, we were marched back through the soldiers, and unto the plane for the remainder of our flight. That was one of the two instances in my life that make me truly appreciate living in freedom in the United States of America. The other one was when, as a sixteen year old, my twenty-one year old sister and I were stuck in East Germany without proper documents (but that's another story).

When we arrived in Johannesburg, South Africa, the thoughts of the trip were rapidly placed on the back burner, for here we were in a modern city and driving up to a familiar sign, Holiday Inn. Yes, we stayed in a very fancy Holiday Inn in Johannesburg. We ate well, we slept hard, and we loved every minute of it. We did some sightseeing in Johannesburg and were even taken to a gold mine. We actually went down into the gold mine.

Gold mines are so deep that they go below the depth where it is a constant cool temperature, like I had been used to when visiting the coal mines back home in West Virginia. In the gold mines it is hot. The gold seams are not nice and neat like most coal seams either, but follow seemingly random paths, first this way, then that, at all angles to each other. One could imagine that this hot chaos was the entrance to Hell, and men worked down there all day and night.

After a couple of days, we were finally off to "the bush." I don't know about anyone else's, but I'm sure my eyes were twice normal size all throughout that trip. However, as we traveled on the bus towards our destination, just outside Kruger National Park in the Transvaal area of

South Africa adjacent to Mozambique, I was rather disappointed in the scenery. Expecting, as I was, great herds of animals and vast misty mountains, the rolling monotonous shrub land with nary a single antelope was deflating.

After what seemed like days on the bus, we arrived at our camp. This was one of the many privately owned game farms which circle Kruger National Park. The living sections were called rondavels, round clay huts. But these weren't native huts, they were just built to resemble them. These were fully furnished hotel rooms with showers, bathrooms, everything, and air conditioned, the very lap of luxury. It turned out that was exactly what the people on the tour wanted, everyone except me, of course.

After a while, arrangements were made for us to set up camp in the bush. Our camp consisted of tents. We had a tent for each two people. We had a canvass shower stall, where the local boys would heat up water, and fill this can with holes in it, so that you could have a hot shower. We even had one tent that was the bar. The tents were pitched roughly in a circle, with the fire in the middle. You must realize that our camp was only about twenty minutes from the fully equipped game ranch. After the first night, everyone on the tour decided to give up on the tents and stay in the nice comfortable, air conditioned, rondavels. Everyone except me however.

You see, the individual who was with us on the trip, as our guide and local expert, was Mr. Bill York, the Wildlife Director for Lion Country Safari. I wanted to stay in the tents, Bill wanted to stay in the tents, and this was the answer to a prayer. I knew that if I could get Bill to know how sincere I was about getting into the animal business, I could eventually ask him for a job.

Those nights spent around the campfire listening to Bill York tell stories about his life in Africa, and all of his experiences, were just about as close to heaven as this little country boy had ever been. I remember the first night, as we sat around the fire waiting for dark, the boys brought everyone a piece of a log and placed it in front of us, between us and the fire, like a footstool. I asked Bill what these were for, and he said to put my feet up, lean back, and wait. As dusk fell, and we listened to Bill's stories, slowly, out of the corner of my eye I could sense movement on the ground around us. As I focused and as the area of movement got closer to the fire, I could see that what was moving were big black scorpions. They had been drawn from the surrounding bush by the fire.

The boys collected most of them, and got rid of them, but they kept a couple to show us that fascinating ritual the scorpion does if placed in a position where it cannot escape. The boys would build a ring of fire around one scorpion. The scorpion would try to find a way to escape, going all around the ring, stopping just before burning its pincers. After some time, proscribed by the eons, the scorpion would "accept" his inability to escape, and sting himself to death. I had no trouble remembering to check my clothes and boots every morning after our little lesson with the scorpions. By the way, I did find a scorpion in my jacket one morning.

As we sat around the fire, we heard this long extended moaning growl. "Lion," Bill said. Then from the other direction came another moaning growl. It seems that we were camped directly between two lion prides. The sounds would tail off into a series of "woofs," as the dominant males proclaimed their territory. Bill said that the ones who "woofed" the longest were the most dominant. I don't know if it was the scorpions, the lions, or the shower, but, as I have said, everyone but Bill and myself spent the rest of the trip in the rondavels.

The only other incident of note, during our stay in the tents, was the night the herd of wildebeests ran through the camp. It was early one morning, Bill and I were awakened by crashing, and shouts from the boys. It seems that a herd of wildebeests had stumbled into camp, and several of them had gotten caught up in the tent ropes. On further examination, we found that half of the tents had been knocked down, including the bar tent. We went back to sleep, and as Bill snored away, I kept one eye open until the dawn.

The gentleman who was going to organize the capture part of the trip was Dr. Tony Harthoorn, author of the book *The Chemical Capture of Animals*. This book includes data, some of which was to be gathered on our trip, on the tranquilization of wild animals. Dr. Harthoorn was using a new experimental drug called etorphine hydrochloride, commonly called M99. The fascinating thing about this drug is that its effects can be antagonized (counteracted) by a drug called diprenorphine hydrochloride, or M5050. You dart an animal with M99, have it go down, do what you are going to do to it; take measurements, treat some illness, etc.; then you give it the M5050 and it would get up and walk away (sometimes run away, or toward you, or various other possibilities, but those are other stories).

Either I was pushy enough, or maybe Bill respected my desire to stay in the tents rather than the rondavels, but eventually, Bill and Dr. Hartoorn let me be their "gun bearer." They showed me how to assemble, and disassemble, the gun and the tranquilizer darts. They showed me how to mix up the drugs, making certain that I knew that one tiny whiff of the powdered M99 would probably kill me. They then let me make up the darts, and prepare the gun for when they tranquilized animals. I was absolutely in heaven. I thought that if I died right then and there, it was OK, 'cause I had already lived a full life.

I can remember Bill and Dr. Harthoorn telling jokes in Swahili. Everyone in the Land Rover would be looking at each other, because no one else spoke Swahili. Bill would say something, and the two of them would roar with laughter, then Dr. Harthoorn would say something, and they would both roar with laughter. It was great to watch, and after a while, you could almost appreciate the humor, even though you didn't understand a word they were saying. You would catch yourself laughing with them, and then feel pretty silly that you were. They were probably making jokes about us "tourists", now that I think of it.

The intent of the trip was to immobilize white rhinos. But that idea got canned for some reason, and we went out and tranquilized just about what ever we could find. We tranquilized wildebeests, zebras, and giraffes. The giraffes were my favorite because I had been designated the "Head Man." The "Head Man" was the guy who ran over to the giraffe first, and picked his head up as high as he could, so that the giraffe would not regurgitate, and choke himself when he was lying down.

I was ready the first time we went after a giraffe. I was so full of adrenalin that I could have probably chased the giraffe down and wrestled it to the ground. I remember that first one, a big bull. We darted it, and it ran off a short distance. We followed very slowly, so as not to run it any more. Running can sometimes reduce the effects of the drug, and increase the possible problems like overheating, which might be associated with the capture. Finally, we saw the giraffe fall, our driver rushed on up to where it was, and Bill gave me the go-ahead.

I can remember the feeling of being on top of the world as I ran over and picked up the head of this giant wild animal. That thing must have weighed a hundred pounds. I am only five foot six, and that giraffe must have been four feet thick. I had to hold the head up higher than its stomach as it lay there on the ground, so that the stomach contents would not run up the throat and choke it.

I did my best to hold that massive head up near my chest. My right arm was around its horns (not real horns but bony protrusions of the skull covered with hair). My left arm was up under its chin as I cradled that massive head to my chest. There was still quite a bit of face extending to the left, past where my arm was wrapped around it. I can still remember the smell of that animal, a gamey, sweaty, animal smell, that smelled like the most expensive perfume in the world to me at that moment.

Dr. Hartoorn took some measurements and blood samples and finally gave the giraffe the M5050. As it struggled to get to its feet, I stood back sweating. Dirty and worn out, my arms feeling like they were made out of lead, I probably felt as good about myself at that instant, as I have at any other time in my life. When the big bull ran away, he took with him a little piece of Frank Evans' history.

We spent several days riding in the bush, darting animals and sight-seeing. One afternoon, we took a walk in the bush from the campsite. We followed a dried up river bed for a while, so Bill could show us some animal tracks, and tell us stories. We came upon the tracks of a leopard, and Bill Started to follow them. We all followed, most of us having a great time. As we continued to follow these leopard tracks, we headed up into the trees (trees are where leopards live). Someone said (I like to think it was me, but I'm not really certain) "Bill, what happens if we find the leopard?" Bill stopped, thought a minute, turned, and headed off in another direction. We just looked around at each other and followed along behind.

There are two other incidents of note which occurred during our stay at the game ranch. Our driver was a fascinating Afrikaner who, quite appropriately I thought, had very large canine teeth. At the time, I thought how he looked like some kind of cat, thinking back on it now, he really looked like some kind of vampire! This guy was really into photography. He had two cameras with big zoom lenses in a metal case next to him; one camera was filled with black and white film, the other camera was filled with color film. When he would stop to show us something, he would usually take a picture of it. I don't know what he ever did with those pictures, but he must have had some pretty fantastic stuff.

One day we were tooling along a dirt path, when I spotted a huge spider web. Folks, I am talking huge, this thing was every bit of ten feet across. As I stretched my left arm out to point at it (the land rovers were British drive, driver on the right, and of course I always hogged the shotgun seat next to the driver), something whooshed past my outstretched hand. The girl sitting directly behind me screamed, as the driver burst out laughing. I had missed the whole thing, being interested as I was, in this spider web. (I will tell you a little more about my fascination with spiders in chapter 14).

The driver pulled the Land Rover to a stop. I asked the driver what all that was about. Well, the girl still couldn't talk, and when the driver stopped laughing, he said "You were almost bitten by a black mamba." I wondered what the heck was so funny about that. These Afrikaners have some sense of humor. Apparently, mambas stand up like cobras, and will sometimes strike at anything that moves. I seems this mamba had been standing up next to the dirt road, and had struck at my out-stretched hand. Mambas are very aggressive snakes.

Our guide pulled the first aid kit from under the dashboard, opened it and took out a small vial. He said that in that vial was the antivenin to the mamba venom. He had to carry it, he said, because the mamba was the only snake they might encounter that, if you got bitten by one, he couldn't get you back to camp in time to save you. I kept my hands in the Land Rover after that.

The other incident occurred when we were out cruising, looking for animals. We got word over the radio that there was a pride of lions on this big rock, near a place the driver knew. We headed off for this rock, so that we could see our first wild lions. Coming up on the rock at a distance, we could see several brown lumps draped here and there. There was a beautiful green meadow-looking area between where we were, and where the lions were, so our driver started off across it to get us as close as possible.

This "meadow" turned out to be a small swampy area that was without standing water, but was still mud below the grass. As we got about half way across it, and very near the lions, the Land Rover hit an area that was somewhat wetter than the rest of the "meadow", and we sunk in the mud up to our axles. You have to get the picture. Here we are, a group of American tourists, sitting in an *open* land rover, stuck in the mud, with a pride of lions sitting on a rock nearby, watching us.

The driver told us we would have to get out and push the Land Rover out of the mud. I vividly remember the looks on several faces when told of this development. People were looking around as if to say, "Is he talking to me?" "I don't think he's talking to me, is he?" Well, he finally convinced us that we wouldn't be attacked by the lions, but he did not tell us about the mud that we would be dealing with. As we climbed out of the Land Rover, on the side of the Land Rover away from the lions, we sunk in the mud half way up to our knees.

I remember looking at the lions, and noticing that several of them had roused themselves to a standing position, so that they could get a better look at the "action" I suppose. I was hoping that they were just spectators, and not interested participants in the game we were playing. As we slogged and sweated, somehow we managed to push the land rover out of the mud. We all got back in the Rover and were back on our way. We got back to camp, had a shower, and laughed about our experience. I don't recall much humor in the situation while we were wallowing in the mud about to be eaten by lions, but, what the heck.

They staged a nighttime lion feeding for us while we were there. Someone's mule had died, so they drove down and dragged this mule up to this big blind they had built near a large clearing. They cut the mule up a little bit, and left it in the center of this clearing. The blind had these big lights on it and, while we were back at camp eating, they prepared the blind and turned the lights on. After dinner, we all went down and got in the blind to wait. Not long after it got dark, the lions arrived, there must have been twenty or twenty-five of them. They tore into the carcass of that mule like they had not eaten for days (which was probably true). It was a gruesome spectacle under those harsh lights, but a spectacle like those which occur every night somewhere on the African plains.

One day we went into Kruger National Park to sightsee. This was our first opportunity to see elephants. We saw a large group from far away, and got pretty close to two lone bulls. We saw many different kinds of antelope. We saw baboons and birds, some of which were in relatively large groups, but nothing like the scenes we were used to from television. Those huge herds, seen on TV, were found much further north, in the vast plains of Kenya and Tanzania. But most of us were pleased, nevertheless.

I must comment on the food we had while in the bush. When we first arrived at the base camp, we met in the bar to get rested and organized. Around the bar were little bowls, little bowls that, in the U.S., would be full of peanuts, or Pepperidge Farm Goldfish, or something like that. But the little bowls on this bar were full of little tiny bits of jerky—dried spiced meat. The bowls contained tiny pieces of jerky made from the native animals. The jerky was very good, my favorite was the kudu jerky. Everyone tried it. Most said they preferred peanuts.

As we were finishing up our three week trip, we stayed for two days in a pretty fancy game ranch called Mala-Mala. The food at this ranch was probably the best food I have ever eaten. The primary meat was Impala. Impala breed so well in these private reserves, that, if they were not culled, they would soon overpopulate the area upon which they live. So, instead of just shooting the impala and leaving them to the vultures, they eat them. Impala meat is tender, free of fat and absolutely delicious. We had impala steaks, Impala curry, and impala stew, but my favorite was the impala sausage. They would make these sausages out of the natural impala casings, stuffed with seasoned impala meat, and coil them on a big steel grating over an open fire. The taste and texture of those sausages was so profound that I can't eat a sausage to this day and be completely satisfied.

During one of the nights Bill York and I sat around the campfire, I got up the nerve to ask him for a job. I remember saying that I would do anything, clean cages all the time, anything, to get into the animal business. To my surprise, and delight, he said "That would be fine. When can you start?"

As I sat there slack-jawed, he said Lion Country was opening two new parks, one in Texas and one in Georgia, and I could have a job in the one in Georgia. I told him that I needed about a week after we got back, to get my things in order, but would be there as soon as I could. He said fine, and for the rest of the trip I was lifted even higher by the thought of employment in the business I had dreamed about while watching Marlon Perkins on TV all those years. After the trip, I couldn't wait to get packed up. I left my home in West Virginia, (I didn't even have a place to stay in Georgia) and drove into my new life, outside a little town called Jonesboro.

# Chapter 5: Lion Country Hoofstock

Let me introduce you to a character we called Shagnasty, Shag for short. Shag was an adult male white-tailed gnu with a disposition that would make Will Rogers dislike him.

White-tailed gnus have a body like a skinny pony with long legs, and, not surprisingly, a long white tail. The body is the only similarity Shag had with a pony. Attached to this relatively innocuous body, was a head that simply did not fit. The basic structure of the head is somewhat horse-like, but there the similarity ends. The nose is flattened horizontally, creating wide nostrils, with flaps which could almost close their nostrils completely. When white-tailed gnus get mad, they close those flaps and blow through them, making a sound a little like a chain saw (As I have already implied, Shag had the disposition of a chain saw...a demonically possessed chain saw.)

These animals also have horns. These horns are not positioned like most animals' horns. Instead of coming out of the sides of the head, they come out forward, immediately bending straight down and out for half their length, then they bend back up 180 degrees, and the tips end up near the level where they come out of the skull. These horns stick forward somewhat, and are very sharp. Shagnasty, having lived up to his name, had broken both of his horns off at different lengths, and he was only left with rounded stumps. The fact that his horns had been broken off, would turn out to be very advantageous for me.

He was a constant thorn in our side, literally and figuratively, when-ever we tried to work out in the hoofstock section. The moment anyone stopped a vehicle anywhere near his territory, you could be sure Shag would soon be there.

That's a little about Shagnasty. I must pause here to introduce you to Nick Reindl. Nick was a fellow who worked with me at Lion Country. Nick was a really easy-going guy from Minnesota. He was kind of tall and thin, and wouldn't hurt a fly. Nick was given the assistant senior ranger spot, as well as his duties of taking care of the hoofstock. Nick would patrol his sections in one of our famous zebra-striped jeeps. Well that's Nick. Now as to how Nick relates to Shagnasty.

As I have said, I was on foot most of the time when I took care of the elephants at lion country, and consequently, subject to any and all the attentions the animals in the hoofstock section might like to give to me. When I was near the area where Shagnasty hung out, I simply kept the elephants between Shag and me, until I got away from his territory. But sometimes, during days we were closed, or at the end of the day, I would have to walk back up to the office, through the hoofstock sec-tion, without my elephant bodyguards. Most of the time I would catch a ride with the senior ranger, or one of the cat men leaving their section.

One day we had closed for a particularly bad spell of rain. I started out for the road and had just gotten out in the open, when, over a little hill, came Shagnasty. He began to trot toward me. At the same time I spotted Shagnasty, I saw Nick driving along the road in his jeep. Nick saw how close Shagnasty was to me, and began to try to get over to me. He was a couple of hundred feet from me.

Remember, we were in Georgia, and it had been raining for some time. That red Georgia clay was wet, and slippery, so Nick had to get his Jeep into four-wheel drive first, before he could get over to where I was. Meanwhile, I'm slowly backing toward some pines that are about twenty feet behind me. I noticed a small pine tree about ten feet long lying on the ground near my feet. The elephants had broken the tree off from its roots and had eaten the top off of it. I picked it up, and held it up pointing toward the steadily approaching Shagnasty.

In the mean time, Nick was frantically trying to put the Jeep in four wheel drive. He finally succeeded in getting the jeep in gear, pulled off the road, and heading my way just as Shagnasty charged. The ground between the road and me was very rough and washed out. Next to the road was a four foot deep ditch, so Nick had his hands full just maneuvering the Jeep.

I was holding this little tree like a lance, between Shagnasty and myself. When Shagnasty charged, I placed the end of the tree right up to his head. (I had not had time to evaluate the quality of my defense prior to this time.) Well, this little tree exploded like shrapnel as Shag charged through it. The tree had been dead for some time. Pieces of that tree flew everywhere, and I was left holding a piece about twelve inches long. As Shagnasty charged, he dropped to his front knees and lowered his head. White-tailed Gnu do this so that they can hook the points of those upward curving horns into what ever they are fighting. Fortunately for me, as I have said, Shagnasty had broken those sharp points off already.

Shag hit me in the thighs with both of his horns, and knocked me backwards, flat on my back, into the little row of trees. Almost immediately Nick arrived on the scene, and Shagnasty moved away, back towards his area on the other side of the Jeep. Nick, however, didn't see exactly what had happened, because he had been violently thrown around inside the Jeep just getting to me on that washed out Georgia countryside.

Nick pulled to a stop right where the "meeting" between Shagnasty and me had occurred. I had fallen down, and rolled behind one of the larger pine trees, consequently, Nick could not see me from where he stopped. I could see Nick, as I peeked around the tree, and he was looking everywhere for me. He could see Shagnasty off to his right, but he looked panicky because he couldn't see me. Nick jumped out of the Jeep, and looked around frantically for me, even bending down, with one knee in the mud, to look up under the Jeep. After the incident, Nick told me that he was sure that, in his attempt to help me, he had run over me.

I came out from behind the tree I had crawled behind, and when Nick saw me, I have never, in my life, seen anyone as pleased and relieved to see someone as Nick was that day. I wasn't hurt much, just bruised. We had a good laugh at me getting attacked by Shagnasty, and then nearly run over by Nick.

A couple of months after that incident, we found Shagnasty lying dead near a lake outside of his territory. He had been gored to death. Evidently his mean streak took him into another animal's territory, and he lost his last fight. We felt very sad at Shagnasty's death, even though he was a lot of trouble. You get attached to an animal with that much character. We missed his life force and spirit.

When I talk about character in the hoof stock section, I cannot keep from mentioning Jackson, the Ibex. An Ibex is an animal similar to a mountain goat. Ibex stand about two feet tall, and the males have long horns which come up, and curve gracefully back over their bodies. Jackson felt he was the king of the east end of the hoofstock section.

I have even seen him go up to a full grown bull giant eland which stood over six feet tall at the shoulder, and butt him in the leg. He seemed to be saying to the eland "Put 'em up, put 'em up" (like the Cowardly Lion). This particular eland would pretty much ignore this pest raging around his knees, but several of the other animals would spar with Jackson. They would, however, quickly get bored. Jackson was a case. He never got tired of trying to show all the other animals how tough he was. If he ever did get in over his head, however, like with the cape buffalos, he didn't hesitate to use his Ibex agility and quickness to get out while the getting was good.

Momma was a fringe-eared oryx. A fringe-eared oryx is a medium sized antelope. They are mostly brown with black trim. They have a bushy black tail, have a black stripe down their back, a black stripe down either side which connects with a black brisket, black bands around the upper leg, and black outlining a brown H on their faces. They have very long, straight horns which come out of the tops of their heads, and can be used for anything from scratching a hind quarter, to spearing an attacker. They have a long flat face with a wide nose, and large eyes set high up on the head. Their ears are mostly brown, but have a black tip, and from that tip, hairs extend out and down. It is these long ear hairs which give them their name. A fringe-eared oryx looks like a beisa oryx except for these ear tufts. Both look a great deal like their larger cousin, the Gemsbok, as well.

I don't know what Momma's background was, but from the time she arrived, she seemed to take a liking to me. She may have been harassed by some of the other animals, and just felt more comfortable around me and my elephants. She was remarkably tame, and would let me pet her, and even touch her horns. A lot of animals who get tamed down still never like you to touch their horns, unless they wanted to fight with you, like some of our addax did (but that's another story).

Momma would hang around me and the elephants, and would even sleep behind the elephant barn were I stored the hay. By and by, Momma had a baby. In reality, before Momma had her baby, she wasn't called Momma. I think I just used to call her Girl. But after Momma had her baby, and she was a real momma, then I started calling her Momma. It was amazing, but, even from the first day, Momma would let me touch the baby, and not even get upset. I watched that baby grow up until it got big enough that Momma didn't want to have anything to do with it anymore, and then it went off to seek its own fame and fortune with the rest of the hoofstock. Momma hung around with the elephants and me until the day I left Lion Country.

We had five cape buffaloes at Lion Country, two males and three females. (Yes, these were the same ones that tried to chase me off the dam.) One of the males, and two of the females were full grown, the other pair were younger, but still pretty big. We had been aware that the larger of the two females was looking pretty pregnant, and so, we were on the lookout for a baby cape buffalo anytime. I happened to be up near the entrance to the Rhino/Cheetah section, shortly after the cape buffalo had her baby.

The baby cape buffalo was lying in a section of small pine trees near the Rhino/Cheetah section, looking quite comfortable on a bed of pine needles. The mother had just finished cleaning it off, and it looked quite healthy. As the mother started to leave, it struggled to its feet to follow her. The mother showed no interest in it, and walked away. The baby caught up to her and tried to nurse, but she pushed it away with her big broad nose. She wasn't being rough with it, she was simply being firm.

For several hours the baby made many attempts to nurse. However, the mother thwarted each attempt. It appeared that the mother had milk, since her udder had swollen, but she wouldn't let the baby drink. Finally the little thing ran out of steam, and just laid down. The mother came over to it, sniffed it once, and walked away. We continued to watch the baby for another couple of hours, but we decided the mother was not going to take care of it. This kind of thing happens from time to time in the wild.

We made the decision to pull the baby and try to raise it at the Cuddle Corner. The girls at the Cuddle Corner were more than happy to take care of this baby. She was a cute little female, about twenty to twenty-five pounds, and seemed to take to her new mothers right away. She soon learned that the bottle would give her what she had been try-ing, unsuccessfully, to get from her mother all day. Though she was weak, she quickly got much stronger after getting a meal.

For two days this little cape buffalo thrived. She did not seem to be passing any urine or fecal matter though, and the Vet was getting concerned. Finally, on the afternoon of the second day, she quickly sickened, and died that night. She had seemed so healthy that the Vet did an autopsy on her the next day.

It seems that she had been born with a birth defect. Her ureter, and her colon, were completely missing. She had no connection between her bladder or her intestine to the outside of her body. She died of toxemia, due to the build up of wastes in her body. We couldn't tell from looking at this baby that anything was wrong, but the mother apparently knew right away. We sometimes think that mother nature is a hard taskmaster, but we must realize that sometimes it is best to cut your losses and go on with life. It's not easy, and you never get used to it, but it is something that you have to deal with if you are in the animal business.

# Chapter 6: Apes and Monkeys

After I had been at Lion Country for about a year, I decided to see if I could learn more about some of the other animals we had at the park. The ones I was most interested in were the primates. We had constructed a lake on the park, by building a dam (The same dam I call the causeway, where Moja kept the cape buffalo from getting me). We had built four islands in the lake. These islands were to be the homes for some primates from the Yerkes Primate Center in Atlanta. One Island was designated for each of the four species of great apes; Gibbons, Orangutans, Gorillas, and Chimpanzees.

After the islands were built, and readied for their respective primates, Yerkes brought the primates out to their new homes. There was a large troop of gibbons, over twenty. They brought in five orangutans, two males and three females. There was a young pair of gorillas, and four chimpanzees. A fellow named Melvin Richardson was in charge of the primates. Unfortunately for him, the primate job also included taking care of the park's very large bird collection as well, so lots of his time was spent preparing food for, and feeding the birds. I recall the flamingo food was particularly nasty, containing, as it did, this smelly oil we fed the flamingoes to keep them pink.

At about the same time I was wanting to venture out into other areas, Melvin was too. We arranged it so that, every chance we got, we would visit each other's section so that he could learn how to handle the elephants, and I could learn how to handle the primates. After a while, we got to the point where we were comfortable with our level of train-ing, and asked the boss if we could switch jobs every now and then. He said it was OK, and so we did.

Melvin had some interesting associates, just as I did, and I soon learned their idiosyncracies. Old Tuan was the boss of the orangutan island. Of the four chimps on the chimp island, Kelly was an enormous fifteen year old female. She shared the island, briefly with a male of about her age, and two very old females named Gamma and Beulah. The pair of gorillas was young, but had some size to them. The gibbons were mostly shy except for the dominant male. About all he was as interested in was getting on your boat and fighting with you.

As I said, we had five orangutans at lion country, two males and three females. The leader of the group was a two hundred and eighty pound male, named Tuan. Tuan stood about four feet high, that is, if you could get him to stand up, and was a peaceful old monarch who reminded me a lot of Henry the Eighth. He loved his food, and he loved his women.

I can remember climbing up on the island, and sitting down on the ground with the bucket of produce, to wait for the orangs to come over to get fed. Tuan would sit at my right, followed, around in a circle, by the three females and finally, the other smaller male on my left. I would hand the fruit to Tuan, he would inspect it and, if he didn't want it, would pass it on. I can still feel the gentle touch of those massive hands as he took the fruit from me. Each of his fingers would make three of mine. Each hand was a over a foot long, from the base of the palm to the tip of the index finger. They told me at Yerkes Tuan had been in a cage that was exactly twelve feet wide. They said that he could sit in the middle of the cage and touch both sides of it at the same time, with the tips of his middle fingers.

Than had massive cheek and throat pads. The cheek pads hid his one small eye. Tuan had lost one eye, somehow, when he was younger, so he would look at you with that one good eye, apparently with the wisdom of the ages. As Tuan would find some choice morsel, he would stuff it in his mouth, past canine teeth two inches long. Tuan could fit two apples in his mouth at one time, or three bananas sideways. Tuan was awesome. If Tuan didn't share as much food as I thought he should, I would sneak fruit to the other orangs, especially the other male, who was on the bottom of the pecking order. Fortunately, Tuan never seemed to mind my feeding the other orangutans.

The islands, where the apes were kept, had been constructed out of Georgia pine forest. The pines that had been on the island had been knocked down, but left for the apes to climb on. There was one particularly large pine stretched all the way across the orang island, that was one of Tuan's favorite toys. Tuan would go down to the root end of that tree, pick up the whole thing and bounce it on the ground. This is a tree, you must realize, that we had to put in place using a bulldozer. Tuan was incredibly strong.

The day we put the first two chimps onto their island will live forever in my memory. Gamma and Beulah had lived at Yerkes all their lives. For Beulah, that had been forty-five years and for Gamma, fifty years. I think Gamma was the third chimpanzee Dr. Yerkes got for his institute, third after Chim and Panzee. Gamma was a wonderful old lady. She loved everyone. She was always so happy to see you, and would just hug on you, and love you, like she was your grandmother or something. She was, simply, a little old chimp who appreciated anything you did for her.

Beulah, on the other hand, was Gamma's alter ego. If there ever was a Jekyll and Hyde, in two parts, it was Gamma and Beulah. Where Gamma was sweet, Beulah was nasty. Where Gamma loved everything you did for her, Beulah wouldn't get excited about anything, anything, that is, except for the chance to bite somebody.

When we took the cages containing the chimps over to the island, we really didn't know how the chimps were going to react. They hadn't been outside on their own since they were babies in the wild. We opened the cages, and watched as the chimps peeked outside, as if to say, "Hey, somebody! Someone left the door open. You better get over here and close it." Finally they eased their way out of the cages, and tested the ground around them. I will never forget the next scene.

As Gamma came out, she looked up into the beautiful blue, sunlit sky, and got a look on her face of absolute wonder. She started chattering excitedly, not able to keep her eyes from the glory of the sky. She would raise her hands, as if to touch the sky, and walk around in small circles just looking up. Remember, the only "sky" she had seen, for all of her life, had been the top of a cage. She came over to us, like she would do, smiling and making soft throaty sounds, as if to say, "Look, look, isn't it beautiful. Isn't it marvelous." Watching Gamma that day made me appreciate what a joy it is to be free enough to look up and see the sky any time I wanted to.

I think Beulah was just as excited about the whole affair, but she was such a grouch that she just sat up on the top of the island, and snuck a peek at the sky every now and then. She didn't want us to know she was happy about anything. Finally Gamma went up and sat with Beulah. Gamma was still in a state of wonder, but we felt everything was going to be alright with them, so we left.

We eventually got a male on the island, not for breeding with Gamma and Beulah, both were way too old, but simply for the display. He didn't last very long though. Unfortunately for him, we also got a huge female chimp named Kelly. Melvin got along great with Kelly, but I never did feel real comfortable around her. You see, she seemed to me to be as big as I was, and I was pushing two hundred pounds. And if her size wasn't bad enough, chimps are naturally about five times as strong as humans anyway. Kelly was also the smartest chimp I ever saw.

I have no proof of it, but I think that shortly after we put Kelly on the island with Gamma, Beulah, and the male, she threw, or chased, the male in the lake and killed him. You see, the reason that you can keep the great apes on islands, is that they cannot swim. They have a density greater than that of water so, consequently, sink without the opportunity or ability to learn to swim.

One morning, when Melvin was out feeding the primates, he noticed the male chimpanzee was missing from the chimp island. He returned to the Wildlife office area, and arranged for all of the rangers to help search for him. I remember I was walking the edge of the lake, near a little cove, when I spotted the chimp's body, floating face down in the lake near the shore. I walked over to it. His arms were towards the shore, so I grabbed him by his hands to pull him unto the land.

A chimpanzee's hands are prehensile, that means that, as force is exerted on them, they naturally close up. This is a very useful adaptation when you are swinging through the trees. It prevents their hands from opening, as they grab branches when swinging. As I grabbed this chimpanzee's hands and pulled, the natural, physiological, prehensile, system caused his hands to close on mine.

This scared me so badly that I let go and fell backwards, with a splat, onto the mud of the shore. As soon as I figured out why this very dead chimpanzee had just grabbed me, I was able to go back and remove his body from the water. His death was a shame. He had been a good chimp. I still blame Kelly. She was just too much in control of her island for me not to.

One day when I was feeding the chimps, Kelly stole my 10" Buck knife. All of us carried knives in the animal business. For the most part, it was a macho thing, but, as an elephant man, it was good to have something to dissuade an elephant from mashing you against a wall. If you get backed against a wall, you simply put the butt of the knife against the wall, with the point facing the elephant, and, if the knife is long enough, the elephant will back into the point before they squash you. This usually convinces them to stop trying to mash you against the wall.

Back to Kelly. I had been cutting up the fruit that I was feeding to the chimps, and made the mistake of laying my knife down on the edge of the boat. It seems that Kelly had a hankering for that knife for some time, and when she saw her chance to get it, she took it. Well, let me tell you, I was just about as scared as I could be. The thought of a chimpanzee as big and as smart as Kelly was enough to scare most people, but now she had a knife!

Kelly took the knife and ran up the island a ways and sat down with her fruit and, to my shock, started to cut pieces off of an apple, and eat them. Now, you have to get the picture. Here was this enormous chimpanzee, sitting on her island, cutting pieces off of an apple with a ten inch Buck knife, and calmly popping the pieces into her mouth and eating them. To my knowledge, Kelly had never held a knife before, but, apparently from just watching, she knew exactly what it was for. The only thought that was running through my mind was, what if she gets into a fight with the other chimps. She was bad enough with her fangs and strength, now she had a knife. I could just imagine explaining that one to my boss.

The only thing I could figure to do was to use her natural desire to possess things, the same desire that motivated her to steal the knife in the first place, to try to get the knife away from her. I hopped back in the boat, (I had jumped out when she ran up to the top of the island. I don't know what I was thinking. I certainly didn't want to chase a big adult chimpanzee who had a knife.), and off I went to get "things."

When I got to shore I just started gathering anything I could find that I thought might interest her. I got lots of fruit, bunches of bananas, apples and oranges. I found someone's tennis shoes and I took them (they are probably still wondering where their tennis shoes are). I got a piece of rope, a ball, and several other things that are only faded memories. Back to the boat I headed, and back out to Kelly's island (Formerly just the chimp island.).

When I got back near the island, Kelly was sitting in the same place, but as I neared the island she came down to meet me as usual. Fortunately, she was still carrying the knife. I pulled the boat lightly up to the island. Usually I run the boat up on the island some so that it stays there while I am doing the feeding. This time, however, I wanted to be able to make a fast getaway if what I had in mind worked.

Kelly was sitting right next to the boat with the knife in her right hand. I got up into the front of the boat, and sat on the edge of it, with one foot in the boat and one foot on the shore. I began to give Kelly all the things I had brought. I was talking very excitedly like, "Oh Kelly, look what I have for you!" I kept handing her things and she was taking them, getting more and more excited all the time at all the new things she had. When I gave her the first shoe, she really liked it, it was differ-ent. She smelled it, and played with the strings. I kept giving her things and she kept filling her hands, then she started to fill her feet. Then she started to fill her lap. Chimps frequently hold stuff between their belly and their upper leg. In a moment, all of her "storage space" was used up, this was the moment I had been waiting for.

She was beginning to have to make decisions about what she would hold onto and what she would just let drop. Finally, she got to the point where she decided to set the knife down next to her so that she could grab the second shoe. At the moment she set the knife down, I reached down, grabbed the knife, and pushed the boat into the lake with my foot. As soon as I pushed off, Kelly erupted. Things that had just been so important to her were flying everywhere. She was screaming, and throwing things, and jumping up and down. Me, I was just lying in the bottom of the boat, thanking my guardian angel again. As I sat up, the ball whizzed past me, so I decided to let her calm down, and I left.

I didn't land on the island for a few days. I was quite satisfied to get near the island and throw the food unto it, until Kelly forgot about our little knife episode. Eventually I did go back, and our relationship was unchanged from what it was before the knife incident. After that, I cut up the produce *before* I went out to feed the chimps, though.

To give you an idea of just how strong Kelly was, let me tell you about a little "housekeeping" she did one day. When the primate islands were built, concrete catch pens were built on one side of them so that we could capture the animals if necessary, to treat them medically or move them in an emergency. These catchpens were poured reinforced concrete with all of the metal gate mechanisms set in the concrete when it was pored. The gates on the lake side of the pens were operated from the lake side, the gates on the island side of the pens had to be operated from the lake side as well, so that someone could capture one of the apes without having to go onto the island to close a gate.

The gates on the island side of the pens were operated with a sliding mechanism, bolted into the top of the pens. This mechanism consisted of a stainless-steel rod which slid through a square stainless steel tube. This whole structure was fastened to bolts which had been set in the concrete when the concrete was pored, not set in holes drilled into the concrete afterwards. One day, when we went to check on the chimps, we noticed what we thought was a stick up on top of the chimpanzee catch cages. We rode over to the cages in the boat, and discovered that it was the inner gate mechanism, which had been ripped out of the concrete and bent double.

We unbolted the opposite end of this bar and channel mechanism, and took it back to show the rest of the crew. As we stood looking at this piece of twisted stainless steel, we decided to see if we could straighten it. Twelve of us grabbed that stainless steel horseshoe and tried with all of our might to straighten it. It wouldn't budge. Kelly had ripped this thing out of the concrete and bent it double by herself!

One day when I was showing another employee the way we feed the primates at Lion Country, we stopped on the Chimp island and I was describing the chimps and their personalities. Gamma and Beulah were sitting on the wall just adjacent to the dock. I was telling him to be very careful of Beulah because I did not trust her at all. I don't know exactly how the next set of circumstances occurred, but the next thing I know is that this fellow turned around to talk to me about something he had seen off to my right.

As he turned, he backed up, so that his back was very close to Beulah. I said "Watch it, Beulah's right behind you." he said "What?" and just then, I saw Beulah move. I started to grab for him to pull him out of the way, but I was just too slow. Like lightening, Beulah struck. She grabbed this fellow with both hands, and pulled him into her. I saw her mouth open wide, and then she bit down hard, right over this guy's shoulder.

She put her mouth right over the whole shoulder, and I saw those canines sink into flesh. I yelled, and so did he, but Beulah had already let go, and was running over to the other side of the island. This guy was pretty tough, because he didn't fall down, or pass out, or anything, but the sight of his own blood running down his arm caused him some justifiable concern.

We jumped in the boat and I got him back to the main complex. They took him off to the hospital but he was back soon. There had been four clean puncture marks where Beulah's canines had gotten him, but other than that he was OK. He finally did learn the ropes in the primate section, and was able to take care of them by himself. In the animal business, you either overcome those kinds of times, or they overcome you.

One day while feeding the primates, I stopped on the Gorilla island and wanted to see if I could get better acquainted with the two gorillas. The gorillas we had were all fairly shy creatures. They never really did want any close contact with humans, neither peaceful contact nor aggressive contact. This made it somewhat unsatisfying when you were around them, because they just huddled together by themselves, as hidden as they could get.

This particular day, I had pulled my boat up to the dock on the gorilla island. This is the dock which was attached to the catch cage area. It had a concrete pier jutting about one foot over the edge of the lake. I put the food up on the island, and made a couple of attempts to get a little closer to the gorillas. My attempts at interaction did nothing more that to make the gorillas nervous.

I didn't want the gorillas to get too excited and fall in the lake or something, so I turned to leave. I was walking back down to the boat when I heard the rustle of grass and a low growling noise. I turned around and saw the female charging right towards me. I started to back down towards the boat, but realized that I would never make it to the boat in time. I decided to simply stand very still and hope this was a bluff. If all else failed, I could jump in the lake. As I have said, the great apes can't swim. I might have a little trouble swimming myself with my boots on, but that option might be significantly better than facing an angry gorilla.

Just about the time I made the decision that she wasn't going to stop, the gorilla was there. She barreled down on me and screamed as she ran past. As she went past me, she hit me on the chest with both hands. I stumbled backwards, down towards the dock. I teetered on the edge of the dock as I watched her run back up and embrace the male. I got my balance without going into the water, got back into the boat, and decided that I would leave getting acquainted with the gorillas for another day.

At the bottom of the lion section at Lion Country Safari, we built a pond. Within the pond we constructed an island. The intent was to put a small troop of Barbary Apes on that island. Wouldn't that be a nice display right there in the Lion section. Barbary apes are the only primate other than man on the continent of Europe. They live exclusively on the Rock of Gibraltar. A Barbary ape is not an ape at all. It is a fairly large monkey in the macaque family, and it has no tail.

As I have said before, Bill York hired me into the animal business. He is the best animal man I have ever seen, and I admire him greatly. But, on this occasion, his planning didn't work very well. (Sorry, Bill).

We put the Barbary apes on the island and fed them using a small boat we left in the pond. Everything went as planned until one day, after the lions had been introduced into the section, one of the lions got wind of the monkeys. This lion started trotting down towards the pond, which was out of the line of sight of the lions (we weren't totally stupid). When this lion saw the Barbary apes, the trot became a run. The monkeys, in the mean time, had seen the lion and were in an uproar (no pun intended).

As the lion hit the water, on its way to the island, the monkeys hit the water, on their way from the island. You see, monkeys can swim, apes can't. I don't know if the "ape" in the name was the fact which confused the powers that generated this idea, but the result was the same. The lion nearly skipped over onto the island, it was going so fast. But, by the time it got there, the monkeys were long gone. Now, if you try real hard, you can see this scene in your mind. Here are the monkeys, running all over the lion section, and there is a lion, pacing around on the monkey island. What's wrong with this picture?

It was with difficulty that we finally got the lion off the island. No one was interested in getting in the boat, and rowing over to the island to shoo it off. But, eventually, the lion got tired of looking for monkeys, and swam off. That one incident was all it took for the monkeys to decide that they would rather live in the trees than on that island. Try as we might, we couldn't get them to stay on the island. We would feed them on the island. They would swim across, eat, and swim back across and head for the trees.

They did become quite a good display in the trees of the lion section but, as with all of our animals, they had to be medically treated and tested from time to time. The first time we attempted to recapture all of the Barbary Apes was a comedy of errors. We did everything from setting automatic traps to hiding in the bushes with a string tied around a stick which held up a box. We had to catch these animals and do the federally-required testing that we had to do each year.

As it so happened, we finally caught all of the monkeys except for the big male. This is usually the way it happens. He frequently lets the others of his troop take "the point" and so keeps himself out of trouble. We tried and tried, but we couldn't catch him, so we ended up having to tranquilize him with a gun and tranquilizer dart.

He was sitting high up in this small tree, wedged in the crook of a branch. Since I had the most experience with the capture gun, they let me do the shooting. You have to be extremely careful with the dart gun on a small animal, because if you miss and hit the animal in the belly or some other soft spot, you could do it a great deal of damage. However, his butt was hanging out over the branch he was sitting on, so I took aim and fired.

The dart struck home, in the large muscle of his thigh and he gave a holler and jumped up. Surprisingly enough, he didn't take off through the trees, but simply sat back down chattering excitedly, watching us with greater interest. He must have thought he was safe way up in that little tree.

Eventually, the tranquilizer took effect, and he nodded off. He did not fall out of the tree, however, because he had himself wedged into that crook of the branch. We were prepared to catch him with a blanket, which we would stretch between us like the firemen do, but he didn't fall. It looked like we had to go up and get him. I volunteered, and up I went.

Now, I am a short, stocky fellow. I guess I am built somewhat like a monkey so climbing should come naturally to me, right? Wrong. Not only am I somewhat afraid of heights, but the tree he was in was quite small. Oh well, on with the story. I climbed up that tree, and finally got to the spot where the monkey was. I was forced to keep my face right up against him as I climbed up higher, and can remember the clean, squirrel-like smell he had. This smell was nothing like the smell of a monkey who lives in a cage. This was the smell of a healthy monkey, living out a very natural life in a captive environment.

I got my feet secure, then realized that I had not thought about how I was going to get this monkey down. I frequently did things without thinking, as you have found out. Most of the time, it doesn't serve you well to think too hard about what you are about to do when working around wild animals. You might change your mind. This is one of those times when it would have served me to do a bit more planning.

I knew I could throw him down, and have my coworkers catch him in the blanket, but I was up this tree and couldn't help them, and he was bigger than he looked from the ground. He probably weighed forty pounds or more. I then thought of my belt. If I wrapped my belt around his waist, and secured the other end to myself, I could climb back down the tree and everything would be just fine.

I unhooked my belt and pulled it out through the loops in my pants. I wrapped the end of it around the monkey's stomach and looped it through the buckle. I then took the loose end and secured it to one of my belt loops. I lifted the monkey out of his sitting place, and slowly eased him out, and down, so that he was free of the tree. This was no easy task. I had to get forty pounds of dead weight up out of the crook of that branch and out around my body and away from the tree, while trying to hold on for dear life to keep myself from falling out of the tree. I knew that my friends would stand little chance of catching me and the monkey in the blanket if I fell out now.

As I eased the weight of the monkey unto the belt, I realized that, without my belt on, the weight of the monkey was pulling my pants off. As I quickly made my way back down the tree, stopping every so often to pull my pants back up, I wondered what kind of a show I was putting on for my friends below. The laughter and wide grins on the faces of my coworkers when I finally did get down with the monkey were answers to my question. There have been many times during my years in the animal business when I would have loved to have had my actions recorded on film. Not to show anyone, heaven forbid, but to be able to see just how silly, or ridiculous, I really looked.

# Chapter 7: Cats

We had a group of cheetahs at Lion Country which were housed, not surprisingly, in the Rhino/Cheetah section. This group developed into the first successful breeding colony of cheetahs in the United States. We only had one cub born the first year, but the second year we had over a dozen.

One of the ways we kept the Cheetahs healthy was to exercise them. Cheetahs in the wild run down their food. As you probably already know, the cheetah is one of the fastest animals on earth. They are capable of reaching speeds of over sixty miles per hour during short bursts.

In order to keep the cheetahs in good health, we used to tie a piece of meat unto a rope and attach it to the back of a Jeep. As we drove around the section, the cheetahs would chase that piece of meat, and thus get some exercise. This wasn't very successful in the long run though, because the cheetahs would only get up to a slow lope. The Jeeps just couldn't go fast enough inside the Rhino/Cheetah section to give the cheetahs a good run. They would start out very excitedly, but soon get bored with this slow moving game.

In the zoo business, it is not good policy to let the animals eat each other, so we had to feed the carnivores (the meat eaters). We fed them quite well. One of the indicators of this was that they did become a breeding population. Despite this, I guess at least one of them simply missed the thrill of the kill.

One hot Sunday afternoon in Georgia, the park was crowded. Cars were bumper to bumper throughout nearly the whole park. One particular bottleneck occurred at the entrance to the Rhino/Cheetah section. You see, there was an ostrich just outside the section, and there was a cheetah just inside the section. Ostriches are real popular at drive-thru zoos, because if you put your finger up to the window, an ostrich will try to eat it for several minutes. He will peck, and peck, and even, from time to time, act like he is swallowing something. I tell you these are dumb birds.

It seemed this cheetah was watching the ostrich too. When the cars were filing into the Rhino/Cheetah section, as the gate guard opened the gate a little wider to allow for the flow, this cheetah bolted past the guard, much to his dismay. The cheetah brought down this ostrich with one bite, and proceeded to drag the ostrich back into the Rhino/Cheetah section. The guard was so shocked by the whole incident, it wasn't until the cheetah got all the way back into the section that he could react.

The cheetah simply lay down next to the road, and began to consume the ostrich. For as grisly as the scene was, the people in the cars seemed to really enjoy it. We got more positive comments about that particular incident, than about any other single thing that ever happened at Lion Country. The word even got back to the business management of Lion Country, and they asked if it would be possible to do that every Sunday. Bill York informed them that wouldn't be a very good idea, and we were able to leave it at that.

There were several instances of note, during my years in the animal business, concerning lions. It seems that most people don't really think that animals in captivity are still wild. Just because these animals appear to be calm, and there are people all around them in vehicles, doesn't mean they are tame. It just means they are used to people. The craziness is not exclusive to visitors to the park either. I remember a time when one of our lion guys went a little crazy too.

We had as many as 120 lions at Lion Country at one time. They were housed in several holding pens scattered throughout the lion section. They were kept in these pens at night, and let out into specific parts of the lion section during the day. There was a ranger, we called them "cat men", stationed with every pride, sitting in one of our famous, now frequently copied, zebra-striped Jeeps.

One day after the park had closed, I heard a call over the walkie-talkie radios we carried, that they needed help in the lion section. When we heard that kind of call, all of us with vehicles would rush on down to see what was wrong. This particular day happened to be a day when I had been given a truck, so, after finishing putting up the elephants, I drove on down there.

It seems that two of the three cat men had put their prides up, and had each then noticed some other lions roaming the park. When they drove down to the other lion holding pen, they saw the other cat man standing on top of the holding pen, shouting at the top of his voice, waving his arms. He was chasing the lions away from the cage!

He was doing a real good job too, because the lions didn't want to have anything to do with him, and were all over the place. Well, quite frankly, none of the rest of us wanted anything to do with him either. However, during a lull in the tirade, Jimmy Lee, our number one cat man, talked him down. We put him in the jeep, and took him up to the main office. From there he went to the hospital for a nice long rest. We finally got the lions back in, they were as freaked out as we were, and went home after another exciting day in the animal business.

As I said, craziness was not exclusive to the visitors, but visitors sure did some crazy things. One crowded Sunday afternoon, we noticed a car weaving through the hoofstock section. Upon investigation by one of our rangers, it was discovered that this car held two little old ladies, both drunk as skunks. We tried to convince them that they should follow us out of the park, but they wouldn't have it. We decided to keep a close eye on them while they finished their trip through the park, then have security hold them in the parking lot.

We did a real good job of watching them until they got into the lion section. As the ranger went over to help follow them through the section, his lions decided that was their ticket to roam. As he radioed for help in watching the old ladies, he went after his lions. There were lots of people in the park. As help arrived, they began to look for the car the old ladies were in. The car was nowhere to be found. They looked at every car in the lion section. They knew they couldn't have gotten through the lion section yet because it was just too crowded.

As they frantically searched, they saw a large, dark shape, up on a low ridge which separated the lion section into two watersheds. As they drove up to investigate, they saw it was the old ladies' car. As They pulled up, the ladies were walking out of a small group of trees, hanging unto each other, talking and laughing. When one of the rangers got up to where they were, he said "What did you think you are doing. You are supposed to stay on the road, and certainly not get out of your car." They looked at this guy and said, straight out, that they had felt the call of nature, and had gone into the trees to pee.

From the bluff, as the ranger looked around in disbelief, all three prides of lions were visible. These little old ladies had chosen a particularly interesting site to go potty, right in the middle of about 100 lions. We finally got the ladies out of the park. Our sighs of relief were mixed with a great deal of chuckling. We would laugh at the thought of these two drunk little old ladies, then get very introspective at what might have happened had the lions been more interested in them.

This wasn't the only time people chose to take a walk in the lion section. The other major incident occurred at The Wildlife Preserve. I was, for some reason, standing over by the entrance to the lion section one busy afternoon, when the cars came to a stop while people took pictures of lions. I can see the picture now. There was this long line of cars, one after the other, snaking down through the lion section.

The lion section at The Wildlife Preserve was much smaller than the lion section at Lion Country. We usually only had two prides, made up of about forty lions total. The spot where these cars were that day, was an open grassy area between the two prides. As the cars were stopped, I noticed a car door open near the front of the line. A man got out and started walking back past the line of traffic.

As I was running over, hollering at this fellow to get back in his car, another door opened, ten cars back, and this other fellow gets out and walks towards the first guy. They meet halfway down this line of ten cars. In the mean time, I'm still running and shouting. They finally heard me, but they just looked up, and waved. I finally got the message across, that they should get back into their cars right away before they get eaten.

They just looked at me as if I were some kind of nut, turned around, walked slowly back to their cars, and got in. I don't know what goes through people's heads sometimes, but it isn't common sense. I bent over double, breathing a great sigh of relief, and prayed that these two nuts would save their quality time together for somewhere other than the middle of a lion pen.

We did discovered one interesting thing about some of our lions, they had this taste for tires. The first time we found this out was at The Wildlife Preserve shortly after opening the park. One day, this four-wheel drive vehicle came rolling through the park, sitting way up high on these big off-road tires. This was in 1974, before this look became popular, and we were quite impressed. So, apparently, were the lions.

As this vehicle neared the end of the lion section, two of the lions walked slowly over to it. I'm pretty sure it was the DB brothers. A couple of real dingbat cats. The driver of the vehicle stopped, thinking that he was going to get a special show. Well, he did. One of the lions went to the front of the vehicle, and one went to the back. They sauntered up to those big tires, sniffed them, licked them, then bit into them.

The air rushed out of those big tires from holes left by the big canine teeth of the lions. But the lions weren't finished, they thought that was great fun, so, switching tires, proceeded to flatten the other two. This guy started screaming inside his vehicle when he finally figured out what was going on. He started his vehicle up and, on four flat tires, limped out of the park.

As soon as he got outside the animal section, he jumped out of his vehicle and screamed, "You're going to pay for this!" Of course we did, 200 dollars per tire. You see, the tires were brand new, and he still had the receipt. We put up a sign after that, to warn people that if they saw lions going for their tires, that they had better move on.

While I have you thinking about lions, I must tell you a little bit about one of the hazards that is not well publicized concerning lions. Male lions will pee on you. That's right, I said lions will pee on you. You see, lions mark their territory like dogs do. But instead of lifting a leg, they just pee straight backwards, and they are very good marksmen.

When we rangers arrive at the park in the morning, the first one into the lion cages has an interesting rite of passage. Picture this, twenty full-grown lions, three to four hundred pounds or more each, with bladders full from their nightly sleep. Twenty lions who want nothing more than to mark you as their own property.

I tell you the truth, walking down through the lion cages, to check the animals first thing in the morning, is like walking through a shooting gallery. Streams of lion pee are crossing the service area as if there were twenty little kids, with giant squirt guns, doing their best to squirt you in the eye. Well, I guess it is better to get peed on by a lion than eaten by one.

I might mention that lions are very easy to raise in captivity. As a matter of fact, if you don't do something to try to prevent it, you can soon find yourself waist deep in lions, with nowhere to send them. We had lions born at Lion Country and The Wildlife Preserve.

In the beginning, at Lion Country, we welcomed the birth of lion cubs. It was our intention to have some lion cubs in the Cuddle Corner area in the entertainment section, on display for people to see. This worked out quite well until these cubs grew up enough to be too much for the girls at Cuddle Corner to handle. It wasn't that they couldn't handle the lions any better than the cat men, it was that if you had four or five, sixty to seventy pound cats, that all wanted your attention at the same time, it could be dangerous.

I recall one time when we were moving some cubs of just about that size. We were being directed by Jimmy Lee in the move, which required that we carry these cubs outside, and around the back of the Cuddle Corner, to an area where they could be displayed more safely. With a lion cub this large, you just didn't pick him up in your arms like some kind of house cat. They weren't leash trained and wouldn't stand to be herded.

Consequently, what you ended up doing was to grab them by the loose skin of the neck, like their mommas do, and then grab hold of the skin over their rear haunches. Thus, you had two handfuls of skin, and could carry the cubs like they were so much luggage. They didn't seem to mind this too much and, if you held them out away from your body sufficiently, they didn't stick their claws into you for support.

Not surprisingly, it is difficult to hold sixty or seventy pounds of lion cub by the skin, away from your body, for very long. We tried to make the trip a quick as possible, for ourselves as much as for the cubs. I remember, as we passed the row of parked cars behind the Cuddle Corner area carrying our cubs, my left hand lost its grip on the scruff of my lion's neck, and all of a sudden, his front end was loose.

I was now faced with seventy pounds of lion cub, who was now not in a good mood, because I was hanging on to the skin of his butt. As I lost my grip, he laid his ears back and hissed at me. As he started to try to bend around to bite me, I hollered to Jimmy Lee, "What do I do?" Jimmy Lee looked around, saw me about to get eaten up by a lion cub and, with a huge grin on his face, yelled back. "Let him go!"

I was all too happy to comply with the request. After I had done so, however, I realized that my lion cub was now loose in the parking lot. Jimmy Lee hollered, "Keep an eye on him." and hurried his cub into the holding area. In the mean time, my cub had gotten himself up under one of the cars in the parking lot, and seemed to be content to stay there. I was quite content that he stay there also, because I did not cherish the thought of having to chase this lion cub down as it ran through the pine forests of north-central Georgia.

Jimmy Lee finally got over to where I was and reached up under the car and grabbed the cub by the tail. That sort of thing was why I was an elephant man and he was a cat man. He did wonder at some of the things that I would do sometimes, so I guess it all depends on your perspective. He pulled that cub out from under the car and, using that tail as a steering mechanism, guided the cub into the holding area. When he came back out, we all had a good laugh, as Jimmy Lee described the picture he had of me holding on to the butt of that lion cub, with this look of fear on my face, and the cub just about to start eating me, from the legs up.

# Chapter 8: Topsy and Me

In 1974, two years after being hired by Bill York, I got a call from a Mr. Ron Bugosh, who was helping to develop a drive-thru zoo in Maryland, just east of Washington, D.C., for the American Broadcasting Company. He said that they needed a large mammal man, and would I like to come down and talk to the management about a job. I said, "Sure," and made plans to drive down to Ocala, Florida.

The planning stages for this park, The Wildlife Preserve, were being carried out at Florida's Silver Springs, a property then owned by ABC. At Lion Country Safari, we were a pretty scruffy lot. Most of us had beards, and I frequently went around wearing overalls. Well, ABC had a different look in mind.

When I went for the interview, I did wear a suit, but I still had a full beard and fairly long hair. I remember my meeting with the vice-president of ABC's scenic and leisure division, Tom Cavanaugh. He said that my credentials looked very good, and he asked if I was aware that they had a dress and grooming code. I said, "Yes. I don't have any trouble with that." Ron had warned me that the beard would have to go if I got the job. Tom said "Good," stood up, shook my hand (one of the best handshakes I have ever felt), and said "Why don't you call us in about a week."

I went back up to Georgia feeling somewhat confused. I was flattered that ABC would consider me for their park, but was taken aback by the "call us in about a week" nature of the last meeting. Frankly, I had a good job, was very happy doing what I was doing, and wasn't excited about leaving the elephants I had come to know and love. So, I just sat back and waited for whatever was going to happen to happen.

About ten days after my trip to Florida, I received a call from ABC again. They had been waiting for my call, and wanted to know if there was any problem. I said "No. I figured if you wanted me you would call me." I was being pretty cocky, and it got worse. They wanted me to come back down for another interview. I said "OK."

Well, this time I wore my old overalls. I guess I wanted to make sure they knew what they were getting. The look on Tom Cavanaugh's face was very rewarding, but Tom is a pretty sharp cookie. He asked me again if I understood the dress and grooming code. I said I understood. He paused just a moment, for effect, then said that if I wanted the job, it was mine. I said something like, "You've got a deal." We shook hands again, and I was off to Georgia to pack.

I came to respect and admire Tom Cavanaugh. We became good friends, even though he was my boss, many steps up the corporate ladder. He was a man of his word. He respected hard work and gave as good as he got. He was instrumental in taking a raw kid, and turning him into a mature, responsible adult. (Tom, I'm sorry I never did quite get the hang of being a good manager, but you know me, the animals always came first.)

I moved to Ocala to help prepare the animals which would be taken to The Wildlife Preserve. My duties were divided between two sites, Silver Springs, and a holding compound near Clairmont, Florida. At Silver Springs we had some hoof stock waiting to go to The Wildlife Preserve. The Clairmont compound had been built to supply a drive-thru zoo that was being developed down there in Clairmont. When that project fell through, ABC purchased the livestock and equipment with thoughts of moving most of it to the park they were building in Maryland, The Wildlife Preserve. The Clairmont compound housed some lions, a tiger, a couple of jaguars, a hippo, three mountain lions, some assorted hoof stock, and one elephant, Topsy.

The three mountain lions were named PU, Jessie, and Ronald. The tiger's name was Woofer. He was named after the sound they make when they are interested or happy, a kind of purring exhale that, from such a big body, comes out as a deep rumble. He spent most of his time immersed in his bathtub full of water. He was so big, he hung out over both sides of the tub, and drained most of the water out of the tub when he got in it.

The jaguars were named Chico and Princess. Chico was a sweetheart, and I used to enjoy going into the cage and playing with him. He would roll over on his back to have his stomach rubbed. The feel of his fur made me realize just what the attraction was for those misguided souls who would buy a fur coat. It was absolutely luxurious. That is the problem with the spotted and striped cats, people want to wear their skins as much as the animals do and, unfortunately, people usually get what they want. I am extremely happy to see that major strides have been made to reduce or eliminate the sale of the furs from these magnificent cats, but it cannot be stopped until people stop buying them.

Topsy was a thirty year-old Asian female elephant, about eight feet tall. She had been a circus elephant that had developed a stiff left front leg, and consequently couldn't take the strain of performing. She was housed in a large pen made of galvanized pipe within the Clairmont compound.

When I first arrived at the compound, you must remember that I had the reputation of working the largest herd of African elephants in the country. Eighteen were in my herd when it was at its largest. The truth of the matter was that, of the thirty or so elephants I worked, most of them were punks four to six feet tall. There were only two older ones, and they were only about seven feet tall, still teenagers. I had never, in my life, been around an elephant who had been involved in the kind of training that Topsy had been through. She knew a lot more about elephant trainers than I knew about training elephants.

I was pretty scared of her, but I was expected to do my job, so I started working her very carefully. As I sit writing this, I am looking at some pictures taken during the first week of my "getting around" Topsy. I really looked nervous about being next to her, and was staying well back from her head. I look as though I was ready to take off at any move Topsy made. Now that I think back on it, that is exactly what I was ready to do, get out of that pen as quickly as I could. Topsy was an old pro, however, and as soon as I settled down, we got along very well.

We started to move the animals out of the compounds and send them up to the park in Maryland as soon as the holding areas up there were built. I had to wait to be "the last man out," because Topsy was being moved last, and I had to go with Topsy. On the day that we were to move Topsy, I was packed and waiting at the Clairmont compound with my 1970 Buick Riviera. I didn't own a Riviera because animal handlers make a lot of money, quite the contrary, I got the Buick from my parents for a kind of, "no money down" deal, when the elephants at lion country pretty much destroyed my other car.

When the truck, which had been hired to move Topsy and George to Maryland, arrived, I was very concerned, because it was not exactly what I had been expecting. (I forgot to tell you that we were going to pick up George and W. T. Hill on the way to Maryland. Don't worry, you'll meet George and W. T. next chapter.) As you can well imagine, it takes a special kind of truck to haul elephants. Not only is the weight a problem, but these animals can be very destructive and, as with the problem I had with Amos, they can move around, and rock side to side, and cause you a lot of grief when you are traveling down the road at sixty miles an hour.

The truck appeared much too frail, and altogether too tall for our needs, but it was the only one we had, and I had to make the best of it. There was one other problem I had to face if we were going to accomplish this move. I had to get Topsy into the truck and get her chained down. You have to chain elephants down when you travel, because you don't want them moving around trying to get out of the truck while you are moving (or while you are standing still either.) (I didn't have to chain Amos down, because he couldn't move around much in that small crate he was in.)

The problem with chaining Topsy up in the truck was that I would have to get into the cramped quarters of that elephant truck, with an elephant that I had known for just a little while, and bend down up under her to put chains on her feet. I didn't know if she minded being chained or not. This would be the first time I ever chained an elephant in a truck, I didn't know what to expect. (The next time I moved Topsy however, I took a chance and didn`t chain her, but rode with her in the truck bed, on a fairly short trip from the Maryland side of Washington D.C., to the Virginia side of Washington D. C.)

Because the truck was so tall, and because Topsy had that stiff front leg, we had to dig a hole in the sand for the rear wheels of the truck, so that the end of the truck was low enough for Topsy to climb into. This seemed to be no trouble. Digging in the sugar sand of central Florida isn't hard (Unless you are trying to dig a posthole, then the sand keeps filling your posthole up as fast as you remove it.). But, and for those of you who have experienced this, you know what I'm talking about, if you are trying to get traction in sugar sand, you better have a light load, good tires, and a down hill grade. We, however, had none of these conditions after having put the rear tires in the hole, loaded an elephant unto the truck, and tried to drive out with semi-truck highway tires.

After finally convincing Topsy to get into the truck and chaining her down with very little trouble, thank goodness, we were ready to move out. After about an hour of trying to move the truck, we gave up. We were sweaty and dirty and tired. We finally called one of those big interstate wreckers to come out and pull us out of the sand.

Staying on fairly well-packed ground, the operator of the wrecker hooked up his cable, and with the help of the truck driver, pulled the truck out of the sand. Once out of the sand, and after having settled up with the wrecker driver, who now had a story to tell his grandchildren, we moved out. We got out on I-75 and headed north. I followed along behind the elephant truck in my Buick and wondered if that truck would make it all the way to Maryland. I was trying not to think of what kind of trouble George might be when we picked him up in Athens, Georgia, on our way north.

Actually, I should have been more concerned about my Buick than the elephant truck, because at about the intersection of I-75 and I-10, north of Lake City, Florida, my water pump blew. As I stopped the car, I tried my darndest to signal the truck driver that I was in trouble, but he just went on his merry way. I called for help, using one of those emergency callboxes the state of Florida so graciously provides (thank you Florida!). A wrecker arrived and towed me to a garage where the boss said that he could put a new water pump on in just a couple of hours. I said I would appreciate it and he started to work.

As night fell, I wondered about the fate of Topsy and the truck. The driver was probably wondering where I had gotten to, and may even have been a little concerned. When I realized that he was probably already at the zoo in Albany, about two or three hours from where I sat, having a nice dinner and getting ready to hop into a nice cozy motel bed, I thought that maybe he wasn't really concerned about me too much, after all. Good as his word, the service man had the car ready in a couple of hours and off I went again. It was near midnight when I rolled into the Albany Zoo, and no one was in sight. The truck was there, so I just pulled the car up next to it and went to sleep. Fortunately the Buick had been built for comfort.

We all got back together the next morning and, after telling my story, I watched W. T. load George up, and off we went for Maryland. I can still remember the way that truck shook and swayed. It seemed that George would, at any moment, remodel the sides of the truck to suit his personal taste. Sometimes the side would bulge out three feet, and then

George would find something else to do, and the truck would assume its former shape. As much as I worried about that truck and whether it would make it to Maryland, it turned out that I had more trouble with my car than we had with the truck.

# Chapter 9: George

Let me introduce you to my biggest personal challenge, George. George was a bull Asian elephant. He wasn't very old, but stood over seven feet tall, and weighed about 8000 pounds. He had tusks about ten inches long. George was born on May 25, 1965. ABC purchased him on his birthday, eight years later.

I first met George after ABC bought him for the Wildlife Preserve. They sent me to a little zoo in Albany, Georgia to get to know him. The zoo was run by a white haired southern gentleman by the name of W .T. Hill. Mr. Hill was an extremely rare individual, an old elephant man (sorry W. T. for the old part). You see, the life expectancy for elephant men is somewhat less than that for normal individuals like dynamite truck drivers or test pilots. In fact, when I first got into the business, Lloyds of London wouldn't even insure elephant men.

I finally got into Albany and found the zoo, and W. T. took me on the grand tour. W. T. had, besides George, the biggest elephant I had ever seen, I think she was the biggest female Asian elephant in captivity. This giant of an elephant was named Laska. The handler that W. T. had working around Laska, feeding her and cleaning up after her, was a gentleman with only one arm I don't remember how he lost his arm, but the one arm he had left was more than enough to make up for the one he had lost. He could pick up a scoop full of elephant dung (and folks there is plenty to fill up a scoop, when the elephant you are cleaning up after is eleven feet tall) with that one arm and load it into a wheel barrow, by just holding unto the end of the handle, not using any leverage against his forearm. He was a powerful man. Both he and W. T. were laid back southern gentlemen, easy going and slow to rouse.

Laska's pen was a massive structure enclosed in steel I-beams, imbedded in concrete. Even considering this massive structure, you could see where some of the I-beams had been torn out or bent, sometime in the past. All of the housing conditions were soon to change at the Albany zoo, however, because the good citizens of Albany were building a brand new fancy zoo a couple of miles away from the old one. As a matter of fact, I understand that when W. T. walked that giant of an elephant, Laska, down the road those few miles, it was a sight to behold. You see, W. T. wasn't much taller than I am, not that it makes much difference, on way or another, when you are walking beside an elephant that is eleven feet tall.

Back to George. We got over to George's pen, which was an imposing edifice of galvanized pipe. The topmost pipe had triangles of steel welded to it to create a pointed palisade atop the fence. This inward-pointing, serrated fence topping was one mechanism to try to get George to leave the fence alone. As we walked up to the fence, W. T. told me not to get too close yet, because George was liable to grab me, and pull me into the pen with him. W. T. also told me that George had already put thirteen people in the hospital. This was not an extremely comforting fact to consider since this was to be my elephant in a few weeks, but it did make it much easier to obey W. T.'s instructions.

I looked at George, and he looked at me, and I'm sure that I looked like I didn't want anything to do with him, while George looked like he wanted nothing more that to get hold of me. My boss had left it up to me just what I would do when I got to Albany, and when W. T. asked me if I wanted to get some time in with George while I was there, I was very hesitant. Finally I agreed to simply having W. T. bring George out of his enclosure. I was determined not to do anything stupid. This was no time for false bravado.

W. T. brought George out and I "met" him, with W. T. standing right next to George's head just in case. Then I backed off to watch W. T. work, so that I would know what commands George was used to. After a couple of minutes it seemed that George had other things on his mind, and started to ignore W. T.. He would wander off and eat grass, and W. T. would have to go get him. Finally W. T. put him back into his pen and I left.

George was such a bother, that, even on his health certificate and animal transportation papers, the veterinarian wrote:
>"This elephant has proven to be of aggressive
>disposition, especially toward people with whom
>he is not familiar. I would classify him, at the
>present time and without further training, as
>dangerous, and would urge utmost discretion."

That was my George!

W. T.'s ability to control George was not exactly what I had expected from a man with W. T.'s reputation, so I figured that George must just be hard to work. This was not a random thought, considering the thirteen people hospitalized after interacting with George. As I contemplated these thoughts, I reevaluated my profession. Just what in the deuce was I doing about to try to take control of several thousand pounds of hard-headed pachyderm. Was I crazy? Yes! It turned out that George would cause me the greatest worries of any animal I had ever worked, along with about 40% nerve damage in my right arm.

After the trip I mentioned last chapter, which brought Topsy, George, W.T. and myself to the Wildlife Preserve, we unloaded George in the elephant section, and chained him to a tree. The elephant section at the Wildlife Preserve was one mile in circumference. (I know because I rebuilt the fence, inch by inch, after my first year there.) It was completely enclosed by a chain-link fence eight feet high. Inside the chain-link fence was the "elephant-proof" fence. This fence was composed of big telephone poles, sunk in concrete, connected all the way around the section with five strands of elevator cable, each cable about twelve inches apart. The elevator cable had turnbuckles on the ends of it to keep the cables tight. (Ho! Ho! That fence rarely stayed tight what with the elephants climbing on it all the time.)

The section had one area of trees, about one-fourth of the total area. The rest was pasture, except for a pond next to the road. The road ran through the section, and separated the trees and the pasture. At either end of the road was a massive wooden gate attached to the cable fence. This gate opened in the middle and swung inward into the elephant section. There was also a sliding gate through the chain-link fence. At the west end of the section these gates opened into the rhino section. At this gate there was a set of electric cattle guards. At the east end of the section, the gate opened into the African Hoofstock section, and there was just a regular concrete cattle guard there.

For two days W. T., George, and I, got to know each other. W. T. would show me how to work George, but never got very far from us when I was actually doing it. W. T. had to go back to Albany to take care of some business, so he chained George up to a tree, and told me to leave him chained until I was comfortable around him. I said that that was sound advice, and thought to myself that George was going to be chained to that tree for quite some time. We left the section at the end of the day, W. T. heading back to Albany, and me heading off to sleep, and wondering if I would *ever* feel comfortable around George. I was really scared of him.

When I got to work the next morning it seemed that the entire staff of the Wildlife Preserve was waiting up at the main office. I pulled up and said "What's up?" They just kind of looked at each other, and my boss, Tom Cavanaugh, finally said, "George is loose." One of the maintenance guys had been down back, and had seen George loose in the section, and had come back up to ask someone if an elephant was supposed to be loose or not.

I can't possibly explain to you the range of emotions that filled my body at that moment. Fear flashed through me like a knife. The thought of finding another occupation that morning crossed my mind. But in the back of all the fear and trepidation, was the reality that I had a job to do. It was put up or shut up. My boss wanted to know if I wanted to call in the vet and tranquilize George. I though about it for a moment and said "No." I said "Lets go," and we got in the jeep and headed out. The entire staff followed us down to the elephant section. There was a breathless anticipation, sort of like when people are expecting to see a race car accident.

We arrived at the elephant section from the east end. We parked outside the chain-link gate and opened it up fully. George was standing in the middle of the road, about two-thirds of the way down the section, just rocking slowly. You have seen the way elephants rock in the zoo. George was just rocking, and watching to see just what all the commotion was about.

I took a deep breath, and turned to look back at the crowd which had gathered behind me. The scene is indelibly etched in my memory. Some of the faces showed true concern, some simple amusement, and some down right anticipation. I was hoping they were anticipating my successful completion of my task, not some exciting life or death battle between man and elephant.

Tom said "You don't have to do this." I thought for just a moment and then said, "Yes I do." You see, this was one of those major life-changing events people have. Are you going to continue with what you began, or are you going to walk away. I must admit that this challenge was somewhat more than what lots of other people face, but the principle is the same, nevertheless. Everyone has their Georges, and must face up to them from time to time. I bent down, climbed through the massive wooded gates, and I was in the elephant section.

As I stood up, I saw George still rocking away in the middle of the road. The scene was one straight from the movie High Noon. The bad guy standing out in the middle of the street, and the sheriff on his way to meet him, alone, with all the townspeople watching from windows. (It is not coincidental that Ted Svertesky's favorite movie is High Noon. Ted was a good friend, and perhaps the best elephant trainer in the world. You will hear more about Ted.)

I took another deep breath and realized that if I was going to pull this thing off, I couldn't show any fear, and folks, there was plenty of fear to show. So I just, as they wanted Cool Hand Luke to do, (another of Ted's favorite movies), "got my mind right." I started to walk straight toward George in a purposeful manner, not too slow, not too fast. George was watching me intently, ears out. George had stopped rocking.

I walked straight down that road, not knowing exactly what I was going to do. All I knew was that I had to get George chained back up. I walked down that road, and as I got closer to George he curled his trunk up under his chin. As I got close enough, I saw the look in his eyes change from excitement to concern, and I knew I had a chance. All this took just a minute or so, remember.

I walked straight up to George, and stopped only when my nose touched his. His head was bent down, with his trunk balled up under it to the right, a simple twitch of his neck muscles, and I would have flown backward about ten feet (I know from experience), and that would have been the end of that story. George would surely have killed me. No one could have stopped him in time.

However, my bluff worked. I had taken an elephant hook with me but decided not to use it. I grabbed the bottom of George's left ear, pulled, and said "move up," (move up is the elephant command for come with me.) George, much to both our surprises, did just that. I walked him back towards the trees to where he had been chained, turned him around, told him to "steady," (that means stand still), and chained him back up.

I smacked him on the butt with my hand as I walked away and said, "Good boy, George." I did not look back, but I am sure there was a puzzled look in George's eye as I walked away. I walked back down the middle of the road to where the park staff was waiting. I was feeling very light-headed, "adrenalin rush" I think you call it.

As I accepted their congratulations, I climbed back through the wooden gates, got back near the jeep, and my legs went. I collapsed into the jeep and just vibrated for about five minutes. I don't remember the rest of the work that day, I suppose I did some. A friend of mine, Mike Jacobs, with whom I worked at the Wildlife Preserve and Silver Springs, still talks about that day. Mike was the Director of Operations at Silver Springs. Mike remembers lots of interesting times we have had in the zoo business. Mike, like my scars, serves as proof that all of this hasn't been just some fantastic dream.

George broke both of his tusks off about one week apart while he was being kept down in the elephant section. I kept a close watch on the stubs to make certain that they didn't get infected. George never seemed the worse for wear for having broken his tusks, and I keep them as a memento of George to this day, the tusks, and the pain in my right arm.

George being loose that first day was really the only major event with George, except, I guess, for the day he tried to kill me. You see, for a long time after we got George, I was the only one who could take the elephants out of the barn and put them on display. Even when we were closed in the winter, someone could feed the elephants, but couldn't clean their barn. What this meant was that my days off were few and far between. The management had prepared for this contingency by hiring me in a salaried position, consequently, they didn't care how much time I put in. Actually, my boss at that time, Tom Cavanaugh, was concerned about my welfare, and had to make me take a day off when I went too long without one.

As chance would have it, one Sunday, October 19, 1975, to be exact, (Do you think I remember that day, or what?) I was given the day off. The elephants, of course, had to stay in the barn that day. To celebrate my day off, I had gone out to a movie and dinner the night before. It was one of those rare occasions when I got to be a normal human being. I even wore cologne and everything. I had found that, in the animal business, you need to smell the same way all the time, so I never wore anything which might alter my scent. And besides, when the first thing you do in the morning was to shovel a ton of elephant doo-doo, you didn't worry about any potential B.O. which might develop during the day.

I was awakened at about eight thirty in the morning by the telephone ringing. Awakened is not quite the right word for it though. When the phone rang, I would shoot up from where I was lying, and go for the phone like it was a living thing. The phone calls I received at that time, were nearly always bad news. News that would frequently place my health in jeopardy, but calls to which I had to respond, nevertheless. Consequently, over the years, I tended to overreact to the sound of the telephone. It took me nearly five years to reduce the apprehension I felt when the phone rang. I began to appreciate the response my father, an obstetrician, used to have when the phone rang.

Back to our story. Yes, it was bad news again, George was breaking out of the elephant barn. I got up, and got dressed, and got down to the park in just about fifteen minutes. They had the gates manned for me so that I could just drive straight down to the elephant barn without stopping. They knew the potential problem that George on the loose could be. When I got there, George was at the main opening of the elephant barn looking very worked up. The lower of the two planks which we used for the gate to the elephant barn, was broken in two. These planks were seasoned oak, Three inches thick and twelve inches wide. They told me that George had been working on the other one as well, but it was in one piece for now.

Let me describe the elephant barn a little better for you so that what follows will be a little more clear. The barn was made of these hugetele-phone poles standing side by side. The top, back, and one side of the barn were buried in a hill. One side of the huge barn housed elephants. The other side was built the same way, and housed the rhinos. The elephant side had three openings in the front. Two small ones, about eight feet wide, and one larger one, about twelve feet wide.

All three openings had two oak planks, lying sideways across the openings, which slid into steel brackets mounted to the outside of the telephone poles which made up the front wall of the barn. The top of the top plank was about four feet high and the top of the bottom plank was about two feet from the ground. Above the planks was a four inch wide galvanized pipe, fitted into its own bracket at about six feet from the ground. With this setup, when I came up to the barn, the top plank would be at about chest high to me, and the pipe was over my head, remember, I am only five foot six. This information is critical so that you can picture the scene which took place next.

I got out of my car, and walked up to the barn. Two of the other rangers were there. They had been assigned the duty of watching George, and seeing which way he went if he got loose. They had been watching George, and urged me to be careful. I told them that if George got me in the pen that they were to do anything they had to do to pull me out without getting snatched themselves. I told them that even if they had to stick a rake in my leg to drag me out that they were to go ahead and do it. It was better to have holes in my leg and survive than it was to be dead.

Let's step back from this scene for a moment and see what the sit-uation was. Here I was, dressed in my street clothes, George had never seen me without my uniform on, and had never known me to smell of cologne, because I had never worn cologne to work before. George had been breaking out of his barn, and knew full well what he was doing, and had probably been harassed all morning (in an effort to keep him in the barn) by people who weren't his trainers. So George was pretty wired.

Alright, back to the past. I walked up to George and proceeded to give him the usual elephant greeting. Elephants frequently greet by smelling each other's mouths and touching each other's tongues with their trunks. Not having a trunk, I just used to pat them on the tongue with my hand. Their response was significantly disgusting to most people. You see, they would put the end of their trunk all over my face. And believe me, you don't want me to tell you where that trunk had been all night! Well, disgusting or not, I used to do it. Come to think of it I used to do some pretty disgusting things quite often back then. But those are several other stories.

George lifted his trunk for me to pat his tongue as usual. With my right hand I reached up and patted his tongue and, quick as a snake, he clamped down on my hand with his mouth. An elephant doesn't have any front teeth except the tusks, which are second incisors, so he didn't do my hand any significant damage by just clamping down on it. He did, however, have me in an unbreakable grip. Had he had teeth where my hand was, he would have simply crushed my hand to pulp. Remember, they frequently eat bark and branches, and have immensely powerful jaws.

At the same time that George clamped down, he rocked his weight back on his hind legs and tried to pull me into the barn with him. Had he been successful, he would have done a head stand on me and crushed me to death. That is how most elephants kill. That cute trick they do in the circus, when the elephant goes down on his nose, with his front legs bent, and then brings all of his body up so that his back legs are in the air and he is balanced on the base of his trunk, that is the killing position. As he pulled back, my chest crashed into the top plank, just under my right arm. The impact was tremendous, but it gave me a second to hook my right leg around the bottom plank, which had been broken double by George, and was now right at my feet.

George, unable to pull me into the barn with his first pull, decided to try to jar me loose. He drove forward with all his weight, and caught my arm between him and the plank. In this position, I was standing with my right leg wrapped around the broken bottom plank, my left hand pushing against the top plank to try to pull myself away, and my right arm twisted and trapped between the inside of the top plank and George's face.

Once more George rocked back and tried to pull me in. Why he didn't succeed is more than I can explain, because he could have literally ripped my arm off. The strain was unbelievable, but I knew that if I let up, I was dead. George drove my arm into the plank again, and pulled back. That was when George made his mistake. It was, for me, a life-saving mistake, but it cost him his plaything. After George pulled back a third time, he made a move to get a better grip on my hand. He came around with his trunk, to shove my hand further into his mouth. As he did, he opened his jaws just a little, this resulted in him loosening the grip he had on my hand, ever so slightly.

It was enough. I had been pulling backwards with all my strength, and pushing with my free hand. When George let up, I actually flew backwards. I flew back so hard that I came loose of the bottom plank and was thrown out of George's reach. Nevertheless, I scrambled back to the truck where the other rangers sat wide-eyed and terrified. This whole thing had happened so fast that they had not even had a chance to get out of the truck.

At that point, we called the office. I got the tranquilizer gun, and tranquilized George enough so that I could get in the barn and chain him up for the night. After I chained him up, it was off to the hospital where the doctor who treated me reported that I had "strained my arm."

Nothing was broken, even though the arm was swollen to about twice it's normal size. There was a compression hole big enough to stick your finger in, in the muscle under my arm, the triceps. This hole was caused by the action of the pressure of George on the flesh of my arm, as he pushed it down over the wooden plank. Kind of like pinching a hole in my arm. The tendons of my forearm had been dragged across that plank so hard, that the tendon sheaths had rolled up, and I had a row of little bumps up near my right hand, one at the end of each of the tendons. The elbow sustained quite a bit of nerve and tendon damage as well but, if I don't bowl too many games in a row, it feels fine.

The next day it was off to work as usual. I went down to the elephant barn, went inside, unchained George, and went about my business as usual. That was the only time George ever hurt me badly, and believe me, I gave him plenty of opportunities. I used to lie down on the ground and have George lie down on top of me. You have probably seen elephant handlers do this in the circus. My legs would be up under his "arm pits," and the rest of my body completely covered by his head and neck. Of course, there was the time I was riding him he threw me off of his back unto the middle of the road just for fun. But I didn't get hurt badly that time.

Before George and I had our tug-or-war with my arm he attacked and injured a young fellow I was training. This guy was a super nice kid. I was always on the lookout for someone I could train to take care of the elephants for me, so that I could get a more normal schedule. Finally, this real great kid showed an interest in getting around the elephants. He was a good kid, and after a couple of weeks, I was feeling real good about how he was shaping up. Little did I know that George was just playing a waiting game with him.

One day I was working with him, and had walked up to the other end of the elephant section to watch him work, when I saw George turn on him and start to attack. I immediately took off running towards them screaming for George to stop. I ran and screamed for what seemed like an eternity. I watched as George knocked this kid down, then ran over him, and kicked him around with all four feet, like he was a soccer ball or something.

I saw the kid go limp and stretch out, just as George turned around and began to do a head-stand on him. All the time I was getting closer and closer but getting no response from George. George went up to head stand on him just as I got there, and my voice finally penetrated the killing fog that held George. George got up quickly and ran up the hill where he stood rocking excitedly. I turned to help the kid and I have never seen a human being as white as that boy was that day.

I had been calling on the two-way radio as I ran, and soon the emergency unit arrived. The kid was understandably very shocky, and had a mouth full of dirt, but was otherwise in pretty good shape physically. George had missed on his head stand, and placed most of his weight between the kid's legs, and consequently, avoided doing him any major physical damage. The psychological effects were, however, profound.

The kid was tough though. He came back to work about a week later, but didn't want anything to do with elephants after that. Believe me, I can understand exactly where he was coming from. We remained friends while we worked at the wildlife preserve. Fortunately for me, he didn't hold a grudge against me. I don't think I can say the same thing about how he felt about George, though.

I finally did get someone to take the challenge again and this time it was a success. Gary Malstrom (It takes a kind of stormy individual to work elephants) succeeded where so many had failed, this relief made it possible for me to move up in the animal business by making it possible for me to leave the constant supervision the elephants demanded of me.

There are a few other short visions of George I would like to leave you with. George was always getting into trouble. He was so mischievous that if you let him out of your sight for just a second, he was into something. For instance, one day he drank about a gallon of asphalt the fence painter had left, and we had to take care of him for that. I gave him mineral oil, and had to clean the asphalt from his trunk and mouth. He thought it was all great sport, and never showed signs of any adverse effects from it. It seems that he was as hard-stomached as he was hard-headed.

One day I had been otherwise occupied by something, when I turned around and George was gone. I hollered for him, and got no reply. I ran up to the top of the elephant section. This was the only place where I could see the entire elephant section. I looked over the hill and, sure enough, there was George, up by this big electric transformer box. It was one of those big green square boxes that house the main electric transformers. They are full of oil which, I guess, acts as some kind of a heat dissipation device. Anyway, these things are heavy, over 1000 pounds, and bolted to a concrete slab. They also had about 30,000 volts running into them, from a cable which came up through the concrete base, and into the box from below.

When I got up to the top of the hill, here was George rocking that big square box up and down, banging it against its concrete slab. Every time he lifted it, I could see the huge power cable running up into it from below. He had broken the box right off of the concrete slab to which it had been attached. I yelled at George to stop and he looked at me as if to say "Stop what?" I ran him off and called the power company. When they came to remount the box, I suggested they fasten it down a little more securely. They suggested that I keep my elephants off of their box.

The day I was injured, when George was trying to escape, was not the first time he tried to break out of the barn. And, on at least one other occasion, he succeeded. He got loose one night. The planks and pipes at the elephant barn had long bolts which fastened them to the barn itself. The bolts had nuts fastened to them. When we put the elephants up, a cotter pin was placed through the bolt so that the elephants wouldn't simply unscrew the bolt, something they loved to do.

One morning I went down to the elephant barn as usual, only to find the planks out, but the elephants standing in the barn as if to say "We don't know who took the planks down!" On closer inspection, I discovered the cotter pins had been removed from the bolts, the nuts removed, the bolts removed, and the planks thrown open—by the elephants.

It seems that George had a fine old time out playing that night. The construction crew had left a dump truck and a backhoe out in the elephant section where they were going to continue to work on the section the next day. It seems that George had great fun destroying what he could of those two vehicles. The backhoe rear scoop had been pushed from a straight back position to a position where it rested perpendicular to the machine. All of the levers had been broken off of the backhoe and the seat was gone.

The dump truck had also taken a lot of damage. Both running boards were broken off, both side mirrors had been ripped off, both side windows were broken out, and it looked as if someone had taken a sledge hammer to any sheet metal that was exposed. The construction company wasn't too happy about the whole thing, but they weren't about to make a fuss personally, to the individual responsible. I put little locks through the bolts in the gates after that incident. It was up to George, and the rest of them to actually *break out* after that, they could no longer finesse their way out. I wasn't stupid enough to leave the keys down at the elephant barn.

The Wildlife Preserve was a drive thru-zoo the first year it was open, and I remember one busy day when the cars were nearly bumper to bumper, George was out in the road trying to see what he could get into. I let him be up there because he was such a great show. The people love being so close to such a big animal. As it happened, I got to talking with some of the people in one of the cars, and took my eyes off of George for just a moment.

My attention was grabbed a moment later by the sound of an automobile horn, followed by cries of help. I turned to look, and there was

George, sitting down on the front end of a car full of hysterical people. It struck me so funny at the time, that I couldn't say anything right away. When I finally got my voice back, the bottom of the front of the car was touching the ground. I yelled at George, who immediately stood back up and turned to look at me as if to say, "Yes what can I do for you?"

I walked over to talk to the people whose hood was significantly dented, and found out that they had pulled up right behind George and honked their horn to try to make him get out of the way. Apparently George had looked around and just slowly sat down on their car, ignoring all of the maniacal entreaties to stop. As you can well imagine, the insurance bill for one of these types of parks is astronomical.

Down in the elephant section was this tree stump and root ball that had been left from the construction of the elephant section. It was about five feet across in every dimension. It had several large roots protruding a short distance from the main ball. Several of us attempted to roll it one day, and could not even budge it. We had attempted to roll it to see just how heavy it was, because you see, George used to play with that giant ball. He would roll it up into the middle of the road in order to stop cars so he could play with them. I would have to make him stop trying to eat the car, then get him to roll his "toy" out of the middle of the road so that the traffic could continue to move along.

One day, George had been down at the very bottom of the elephant section where the chute was located which led to the gate to the elephant barn. It was through this area that I would walk the elephants to put them out in the morning, or put them up at night. This area was a rather narrow one, designed to funnel animals toward the gate. As I said, one day George was hanging around down there, probably thinking up some new mischief, when Bob and Carol, two of our rhinos, strolled down in behind him to see what was up. (You will meet Bob and Carol later.)

The rhinos were kept in the elephant section after we gave up trying to keep them in their own section (you will find out why later also). George was standing down by the gate, facing away from the section. Apparently George was really lost in thought and so didn't see the rhinos move in right directly behind him. The rhinos were simply trying to figure out what was going on. They are very curious animals.

When George finally realized that there were two rhinos directly behind him, he went crazy. You seee, the rhinos had him trapped in the chute. He started kicking backwards like some berserk boxer. The rhinos had situated themselves so that one was behind each of George's back legs. As George would kick back, he would catch one or other of the rhinos up under the chin, and lift it's head up with the "uppercut."

Rhinos aren't very smart, and it took several seconds before they realized what was happening. In the meantime, George was getting more and more scared, and hopping back and forth on his hind legs, kicking, like some giant gray tango dancer. The rhinos finally got the message and started to back up out of the chute. There wasn't room enough for them to turn around. As the rhinos backed up, George backed up with them, kicking all the time.

It was a strange scene. These two big rhinos being punched in the chin by this out of control elephant, all of whom were backing up slowly, trying to find a way out of their predicament. As they got to an area where they could turn, the rhinos took off. George backed up to a point where he could turn around and, looking very carefully, turned, and ran up to the end of the elephant section opposite of where the rhinos now were. George spent several minutes growling and carrying on. It must be quite embarrassing to be that big and experience that big a scare.

Elephants use all of their senses to communicate. They have fairly good eyesight. They use their sense of smell constantly, and have distinctive scent recognition systems. They use their sense of touch to identify and orient. They even taste the characteristic oils which come from the temporal glands of the elephants they meet. And finally, they have extremely well developed vocalizations. I have recently seen research which has "discovered" that elephants communicate with tones too low for the human ear to detect.

I put the word discover in quotation marks because elephant men have know of this low register vocalization for years. All you have to do is to hug the leg of an elephant and you can feel the vibrations in your own chest. These vocalizations may have played a role in the amazing communication George and Topsy had with each other.

Frequently, when I was in the elephant barn at the Wildlife Preserve, George and Topsy would play a game they really enjoyed. While I was inside the barn shoveling elephant doo-doo, and not paying a great deal of attention to the elephants, (you get that way after a while), George and Topsy would play with me.

George would, very carefully, back up near me and step on my foot with one of his rear feet. There are two factors I have to clear up before I go on. First of all, it wasn't unusual for the elephants to brush me or bump into me as I worked. As I have said, they use their sense of touch for fine orienting. They have sparse hairs all over their bodies and, with the sensory input from them, can tell where the boundaries of their massive bodies are at all times. You have to have some system when you have so much body to account for, and such little eyes to account for it.

The other factor I must mention is that, when an elephant steps on your foot, it isn't as bad as you might imagine. The foot of an elephant is designed to cushion their massive weight. Consequently, it is composed mostly of fatty tissue, which spreads when they put their weight on it. So, when an elephant steps on your foot, the tissues give somewhat and mold around your foot. It isn't like being stepped on by a horse, for instance. A horse has a hard hoof which puts the weight of the animal over a very small area, and can be very damaging.

When an elephant does step on you, although it doesn't cut you like a horse's hoof, it does distribute a great deal of weight on your foot. The joint which connects my left big toe to my foot grew to about twice the

normal size due to the forcible separation of the joint caused by elephants stepping on my foot. I have since had surgery to repair the joint.
There was, in fact, a piece of bone that had been broken off by the
elephants which had to be removed along with the joint repair. My
doctor says my right foot should last a few years longer.

OK, with those two pieces of information, let's get back to our story.
George would slowly, premeditatedly, back up until he could step on
my foot. He would step on my foot, effectively pinning me to the
elephant barn floor. Then, by some means beyond my ability to detect,
he would signal Topsy, and she would back up against my back, and
sandwich me between herself and George. They may have been using
that sub-auditory communication I spoke of, but, however they did it
they did it often and quite successfully.

Now, let me paint you the picture which resulted from the actions of
these two multi-tonned scamps. There I was, five foot six, sandwiched
between two large gray masses…two elephant butts, seven feet tall and
four or five feet wide. I guess if I had a picture of that scene it would
look like two elephants, butt to butt, with little arms sticking out the
sides between them, and little legs sticking out below them. It would
probably look like a Farside cartoon.

George and Topsy would just hold me there, not trying to squash me or
anything, (they could have if they had wanted to). I would yell at them and
pound on George's butt with my fists (something which only served to
abrade the skin off my hands). They would hold me there for several minutes at a time. Then, on some unknown signal, they would simply release
me and go on about their business as if nothing had happened.

I would have given anything to have been able to get inside those
elephants' minds at a time like that. Most people who try to find a
major difference between animals and man will frequently site
humor as the one thing man has that animals don't. Well, I can tell

you from personal experience, that these two elephants knew the power of a good joke.

George also turned out to be ticklish. Sometimes when I would come up to him and dig into his side with my fingertips like I was tickling him, he would bend all over towards me, and shake, and make all kinds of strange noises with his trunk. If I stopped, he would look over at me, not moving, as if to say "Hey, what did you stop for?" Then, if I continued, he would shake, and "laugh" till he couldn't stand it anymore.

One day, however, George wasn't laughing and neither did I. George had been getting into something, as usual. I don't know what it was on this occasion, there were so many little incidents like stealing hats from people if they rolled their windows down in the elephant section. That is were I got several of the hats in my hat collection.

On this particular day, however, I was yelling at George for something. I was up in his face, facing him, and he had his trunk coiled up under his right jaw just like the first day I had to chain him up alone. As I yelled at him, I must have made a quick move. George, thinking that I was going to hit him or something, reacted instinctively. He raised his head with a snap and shot out that trunk, still balled up on the end.

That balled up mass of muscle hit me on the left side of my face with all the power George had stored in his neck and trunk muscles. You have seen cartoons where people have been hit and have flown backwards several feet, well, this was no cartoon. I became airborne, and landed slap on my butt, ten feet from where I had been standing. George, upon realizing he had just punched his master, screamed, and ran off to the top of the elephant section, peeing all over himself.

I got up and dusted myself off. As I brought my hand up to my face, which really stung, it came away bloody. An elephant's hide is rough, like course sandpaper. George had, in the instant he hit me, effectively sanded my face. The whole left side of my face was raw. George had peeled the first couple of layers of skin off of me.

I was really mad. I looked for something to hit George with and picked up a piece of chain. As I said, George had split the minute I hit the ground. He was running through the elephant section towards the pasture area. I started running and screaming at him. I had to convince him that he could not hit me any time he wanted. Otherwise, he may get it in his mind that I was no longer the boss. It is a mental game you must play with elephants. Clearly, the physical game was one you could not win.

So I ran after George swinging this piece of chain. I was so mad I didn't think about what I was doing (again). As I would swing this chain at George's butt, all I succeeded in doing was whacking myself with the chain. I hit myself on both legs and both arms. I even hit myself in the back of the head once. My right hand, the one holding the chain, was all cut up and bruised. I finally figured out I was doing a lot more damage to myself than I ever could have done to George, so I stopped.

I went down to the barn and washed my face (which really felt good, ha, ha) and went back up to get George, my anger abated somewhat by the stinging of my face. He was so scared of what I was going to do to him, it took me the better part of an hour before I could even get close to him. When I see that aftershave commercial which says "Thanks I needed that," I think about how I did not need the sort of "refreshing" awakening I got when I had splashed that water on my raw face.

That's George. With George it was always "The best of times, and the worst of times." You have mostly heard about the "worst of times," but George gave me great pleasure as well. It was thrilling to have control over such a large, independent animal. Also, despite our run-ins, George and I really liked each other. I miss George from time to time, and, even though he gave me pain to remember him by, I bear no grudges. George was George, no more, no less. He was that immovable object to my irresistible force. We were well suited to each other, and we both grew from the experience. I understand that George is now giving little kids rides at carnivals and fairs. Oh, George, have we come a long way!

# Chapter 10: Wildlife Preserve Punks

I had eight punks at the Wildlife Preserve, five females and three males. Their names were Rosemary, Sage, Hisani (yes the same one I had at Lion Country), Timba, Kenya, Tanish, and Vaal, all African elephants, and finally Gabriel, a young Asian male. Rosemary and Sage had been housed down at the compound at Silver Springs while the Wildlife Preserve was being built. Gabriel arrived at The wildlife preserve a short time after we had gotten the others.

Rosemary was a snotty, hard-headed little female punk. She made it easy for me to understand why we call them punks. She was always picking on Sage and I had to keep an eye on her to make sure she didn't get into anything. She was very healthy and plump, and was about five years old when we got her.

Sage was a pitiful little female elephant. She was skinny, and her ears had turned over at the top. Rosemary had made her so nervous that she was very hard to get around. She really craved attention though, and you could see her wrestle with the desire to have the attention while trying to control her fear. She was very much like Hisani, from Lion Country in that respect, and oddly enough, Hisani was one of the elephants I bought to bring up to The Wildlife Preserve.

I have spoken of Hisani, but with her arrival at the wildlife preserve, and her acquaintance with Sage, she came out of her shell quite a bit. The trip in the truck, the new surroundings, and the new elephants, all acted to give her more confidence that she had at Lion country.

Timba was a very nice male elephant with pretty nice tusks. He was quite handleable and easy to work. One of his ears had turned over at the top, so he wasn't quite as good looking as he could have been, but he made up for it with his good disposition. He used to like to play/fight with George all the time. George would be surprisingly gentle with him, and he really seemed to enjoy playing.

Kenya was a good looking little male with tusks even bigger than Timba's. Timba was no trouble but, by the same token, he wasn't very easy to get real familiar with. He always seemed to maintain his psychological distance, no matter what.

Tanish was a very nice looking little female. She reminded me somewhat of Shalati. She was easy to work, did what you wanted her to do, and never caused any trouble.

Vaal was a young female who, like Tanish was kind of low key, and never caused much trouble. She got along well with the other elephants and seemed to enjoy her lot in life.

Gabriel was a little Asian male born in the Portland Zoo in Portland, Oregon. He was well trained, and came with lots of equipment with which to perform. He responded to many commands and was fairly easy to work with. It took me a while to get around him completely, but after that we became good friends.

I was even able to have Gabriel participate in the Saint Patrick's Day parade through downtown Washington, D. C.. We walked the whole parade route, through shouting people, motorcycle policemen, and other parade participants. Gabriel wore a large, Kelly green Leprechaun's hat and a big Kelly green bow tie. I have never liked dressing animals up, but I must admit Gabriel looked pretty cute with that hat and bow tie on.

Sometimes, at The Wildlife Preserve, a thunderstorm would come up while the elephants were on display. Thunderstorms came up at Lion Country as well, but in the Georgia clay, the elephants simply liked to play in the mud, they did not do so in Maryland. At the Wildlife Preserve, the elephants would get very nervous at the crack of lightening and the roll of thunder. I found that if I sat down on a fallen log in the grove of trees in the elephant section, and softly played my harmonica, the elephants would gather around and calm down, softly rumbling to each other. You have all heard the quotation "Music hath charms to soothe the savage breast" (yes breast, not beast). Even though my harmonica playing skills are, to say the least, poor, they seemed sufficient to soothe those "savage breasts."

While I was working the elephants at the Wildlife Preserve, the management came up with this wonderfully hair-brained (sorry Tom) idea.:The Nighttime Safari. During the second year at the Wildlife Preserve, the management decided to purchase these large bus-like trams to carry the people through the animal sections, instead of letting the people drive their own cars. These trams were a good idea in principle, but had some problems from time to time. I remember when the big-wigs at ABC came down to take their first ride on the trams. The air conditioning broke down on the tram they were in. When they got around the park to where I was, I could see through the windows the red, sweaty faces of some very unhappy, very important people. But back to the night-time safari.

The park equipped the trams with these huge lights, mounted on the top of the trams, and powered by their own generators. The trams would travel through the park after dark, carrying people into the exciting world of "animals after dark." The Night-Time Safari only took place on Thursday, Friday and Saturday nights. One of the reasons for the failure of The Night-Time Safari, was that no one told the animals they were supposed to be exciting at night. The bears, wolves, rhinos, elephants, and lions had been used to being put up in their cages at about six o'clock, and were noticeably unwilling to have to perform for another six hours.

Another problem with The Nighttime Safari was that someone had to stay out with the elephants. The elephants had to be kept on display, and be kept from getting into mischief (You have already met George!). Guess who got that job. I must admit that Tom Cavanaugh did come to me to ask me about the feasibility of the project, but, as I have said, Tom is a pretty sharp cookie. He knew that I couldn't turn down a challenge. We did have to make a change in my schedule, however. Since I had to be at work at about eight o'clock in the morning, and since I wouldn't be getting off work until one the following morning, Tom graciously let me have the other four days of the week off.

The schedule was great for me, because there had been many days when I had worked those kinds of hours and not gotten any days off. (They saw me coming, and hired me on salary. There were times when my hourly employees were making three times as much money as I was.) Anyway, I would work for three long days and sleep the following day, then I had three more days off. It was like having a vacation every week. It was short lived, however, because The Nighttime Safari only lasted about six weeks.

Let me paint you the picture of a night of Nighttime Safari. I was out in the elephant section. By the way, I think I forget to mention that the elephant section was also the hyena section. OK, I was out in the elephant section, on foot, at night, with no lights. I was by myself for four hours, surrounded by eight elephants (one of whom was George remember), four rhinos, and was aware that somewhere in the dark were seven hyenas.

The hyenas' names were J. H., Linda, Lou, Yakky, Chopper, Circe, and Snake. Circe and Snake had been leash trained and, consequently, were pretty handleable, but the others were a pretty hyena-acting bunch. These were striped hyenas, not the ugly spotted hyenas you see in all the African movies (Although these wouldn't win many beauty contests, even with their black and white striped fur). They were, consequently, less dangerous. All of them except for Chopper that is. Chopper was a nut.

I remember the trepidation with which I faced my first night of Nighttime Safari. As darkness fell, the elephants wondered what in the heck was going on. Why weren't they being put back into their nice, safe, comfortable, elephant barn, where the food was waiting. After about an hour of trying to persuade me to open the gate and let them go home, they decided to find other things to do. I found out later that all the animals that were accustomed to being put up when the park closed, were just as confused. The other times when we confused the animals like that, included when we switched back and forth from daylight savings time. The animals would either want to go back up "too soon" in the fall or they were not ready to go up in the spring.

As it got darker, my little flashlight seemed to get more and more insignificant. The night sounds overtook me, and every little noise seemed to be connected directly to my central nervous system. The elephants were restless with these new and unusual demands, and so was I. I didn't know what the hyenas were up to. I did know when the first tram left the entertainment section, however, I could tell it was moving, because the lights of the tram were visible all the way across the park.

One of the things we had not considered was the noise the generators made. This noise chased most of the animals into hiding for the first couple of weeks. As the tram got closer to the elephant section, the elephants got somewhat more nervous. I did my best to quiet them, but this situation was as new to me as it was to them. The tram entered the section, lights blazing and generator roaring, and the elephants got all worked up. It was all I could do to keep them from bolting. They finally calmed down, and simply kept a cautious distance from this new monster in their midst.

The first night of Nighttime Safare was over. It had gone quite well, all things considered. After all, I had survived it so far. Now it was just a matter of putting the animals up, and going home for a short rest before coming back bright and early the next morning. The elephants were quite relieved at finally being able to go to bed, and after locking them in, I went back out in the section to put up the hyenas. I thought that the hyenas should be about ready to go home too, and was quite surprised to find only two of them at the cage entrance. I put those two up and got on my radio to tell them, up front, that I would probably need help putting the hyenas up.

I began searching for the hyenas in their old familiar places. They had dug several dens in out of the way places, and spent most of the days in them, out of the way. You see, hyenas are nocturnal, they are awake at night, and so they never were much of a show. As I said they were nocturnal, so they were not in their usual holes. They had apparently awakened, after a nice long day's sleep, and were ready to party. We looked for about thirty minutes and finally found two more of them. We succeeded in coercing them into their cages. The hyenas were finally having a great time, wandering around at night like they thought they were supposed to.

We were still having trouble finding the other three. I can remember walking along the fence line at the bottom of the elephant section looking for hyenas, and having the unsettling feeling that something was following me. I turned around, and as I brought my flashlight around, there were the other three hyenas, led by nasty boy, Chopper.

It seems that while I was sneaking around trying to find them, they had already found me, and were simply stalking me as I walked. I don't know if they had any ulterior motives, like eating me. But I know that, when I was able to breath regularly and could assess the situation calmly, they didn't seem at all intimidated by my presence. I finally yelled for one of the other rangers. I told him that I had found them, and needed help moving them. After he arrived, the hyenas turned around and we eased them up along the fence line and into their cage.

That was Nighttime Safari. As I said, it didn't last too long, and I was real glad of that. The four days off a week were nice, but the three days on were harrowing. Thinking back on it now, I will never forget those three smiling hyena faces staring out from under my flashlight beam. I'll never know what was on their minds, and perhaps that's for the best.

Now I am going to jump seven years into the future, to tell you a little about the elephants I had at the park named Wild World. (Well, they weren't my elephants, nobody wanted these elephants but Ted Svertesky.) This was a park built on the same sight as The Wildlife Preserve. This park housed many animals, among them The Ringling Bulls. The Ringling Bulls were a group of elephants just too dangerous, or too lame, to be used in the circus any more. So, rather than kill these elephants, Ringling Brothers found someone crazy enough to take care of them.

That someone is Ted Svertesky, the greatest elephant man in the world. (This is the Ted Svertesky mentioned in the chapter on George.) But seriously, no one else was willing to take care of the elephants that Ted took care of. These elephants include Hugo, a huge Asian bull, Vance, another big Asian bull, and not just a little bit insane, Mary, a sweet, tolerant, but dominant, old female who is somewhat lame, and Major, "the baddest little elephant in the whole wide world."

There is an interesting little story which supplied proof to my belief that I lived a life watched over by some higher power. (This belief was supported by many such stories.) One day, before we were open at Wild World, Ted and I went down to the elephant section to rest after a morning of working pretty hard. Ted went into his trailer to watch TV, and I stayed outside, sprawled on a large boulder, and took a nap. The Ringling Bulls were chained up on the hill above the boulder. Just across the road was Ted's trailer, up on a little rise.

Vance, the lunatic, had this uncanny knack of getting loose from his leg chains. It would amaze Ted, and you never knew when chains would hold Vance and when they wouldn't. I had been napping for about thirty minutes when I awoke. I got up and went into Ted's trailer to get something to drink. When I came back from the refrigerator, I looked out the window and saw an elephant coming down the hill. I said to Ted, "What elephant is that, Ted?"

Ted looked out the window and realized that Vance was loose. As we watched, Vance went over to the rock I had been lying on, smelled of it, then climbed up on it with his front end and rested his chest on it. Then he simply got up, and Ted went out and took Vance back up the hill and chained him back up. I don't know what caused me to awaken when I did, or what timing Vance was under, but if either I had risen five minutes later, or Vance had been five minutes early, I would probably be just a grease spot on that rock today.

I have mentioned Major, "the baddest little elephant in the whole wide world." This was the impression Ted had given me, and I was soon to realize that what had he said was true. It had been arranged that Ted and the Ringling Bulls would stay at Wild World. Ted would put on some elephant shows in the entertainment center. Several days had been spent getting the elephant barn in condition for housing the Ringling Bulls. We spent a day in Baltimore getting the proper chains and equipment from the nautical supply houses there. When conditions were as right as Ted could get them, we had the elephants brought in.

Unloading the elephants and putting them in the elephant barn went fairly well, and we were ready to unload the last elephant in the early afternoon. The last elephant was Major, and you couldn't just unload him. For, you see, Ted had to "get around" him first.

"Getting around" an elephant requires that you teach the elephant that you are in control, so that that elephant does not do you an injury. If you don't convince them, mentally, that you are the boss, they won't do what you say. And if they won't do what you say, the very best you can hope for is an elephant out of control. The very worst you can expect is a trip to the funeral parlor, and not as a mourner.

We began to unload Major, which required that the chain on his back leg be loosened from the truck floor and attached to the front of my Blazer. It was my job to maintain control of the rear end of Major while Ted controlled the front end, until we could get Major chained up in the trees, so Ted could "get around" him. As I eased back on the Blazer, to induce Major to back out of the truck, Ted would give Major a little more length of chain from the front of the truck. As luck would have it the front chain came loose somehow, and Major backed out of the truck on his own, secured only by the chain on his rear leg attached to the front of my Blazer. Major looked around with his little ears outstretched. He had only one tusk, and it seemed to act like a radar gun as he searched for "targets".

My thoughts, at the time, centered on the expectation that Major was probably going to open my Blazer like a can of sardines, and consume me. With this in mind, I leaned out the window and, as quietly as I could (I didn't want Major to come to see what I was doing), asked Ted what should I do if Major came toward the Blazer. Ted, in his unpresupposing, not terribly helpful, way said, "Back the Blazer up." That was a great comfort to me, sitting in a sardine can, chained to "the baddest little elephant in the whole wide world."

Ted finally saved me by grabbing the length of chain that was trailing from Major's front leg with a rake, and we finally got Major chained up down in the trees near the elephant barn. Don't think that all this time Major was being a good boy. He was doing his level best to implement a plan which would result in him coming into possession of somebody's body. I was just lucky enough that he didn't realize he already had me on a chain.

It was about four o'clock when everyone else left, except Ted and me. Ted had to "get around" Major, and I was the closest thing Ted could find to a back-up. You must realize that I was under instruction from Ted not to get anywhere near Major. I was there to simply report to the authorities if Ted got killed. Ted worked on Major until it was near dark. I can still hear the echo of Ted's "Lie down Major! Lie down Major! Lie down Major!", as it was repeated time and time again, as Ted tried to get Major to do that one simple thing.

Ted was not completely satisfied with the relationship he had with Major just yet, but we needed to get Major into the elephant barn before dark. Since Ted had not "gotten around" major completely, he decided to try to use another elephant to get major into the barn. This required that I work *that* elephant, while Ted controlled Major. Fortunately for me, there was an elephant suited to the task who would probably do what I said. So we went up to the barn and brought back Mary. Mary was a sweetheart. She had been worked by so many people that she forgave me any mistakes I made, and tolerated my asking her to do things.

Ted and I discussed exactly what we were going to do as we walked up to the barn to get Mary. We were going to chain Major to Mary and unchain Major from the tree. I was going to lead Mary up into the barn, and turn her so that Major would be in his proper position in the barn. All the while, Ted would be trying to keep Major from getting him, or Mary, or me. The one thing we neglected to discuss was the fact that the other elephants were already in the barn, and would this cause any problems? (Well, maybe!)

We got to the barn, unchained Mary, and walked her back down to where Major was. Ted took Mary down near Major and threw a chain around Majors neck. He used Mary to run interference for him while he secured the chain to Major's neck. He then took the chain around Major's neck and chained Major to Mary, with the chain around Mary's neck as well. Mary was on Major's left side. I was on Mary's left side, and Ted was on Major's right side.

Ted then unchained Major from the trees, and I got Mary moving out. Ted had told me, no matter what happened, to keep moving. He said that Mary will lead Major as long as Major didn't have too much time to think about what was going on. So we moved out and were on our way to the barn. Everything was going great until I started up the hill into the barn area. When I looked into the door we were to go through (me first), there was the massive head of semi-stable, partially insane, Vance.

I said, in a voice that (as I think back on it) was extremely high pitched and unsteady, "Ted, Vance is in the way!" The elephant barn was a long structure made out of telephone poles imbedded into a hillside, with only the front poles exposed. In the front of the barn were three gaps, through which you could move the elephants in and out. Ted had chained the other elephants facing the front the barn, with Hugo first on the left, then Vance, then the space for Major, then Mary and so on. We had forgotten that, as I brought Mary up and into the barn, I would have pass right directly in front of Vance. That was not a good place to be. Vance was insane!

It was too late to change anything, so Ted said, "Stay away from Vance." Right, easy for you to say, Ted! I remember as I got closer to the doorway, that I tried to make myself as psychologically small as I could. When I went past Vance, I got as far up under Mary's head as I could without getting too close to Major on the other side. I hurried Mary in. Fortunately, Vance was enjoying the show and did not choose to participate. He just kind of moved his enormous body to his right, and let us come in.

As Vance's massive body went by me on the left, I spun Mary clockwise and Ted backed Major into his place and chained him down. Ted unhitched the two elephants, rechained Mary, and we got out of that barn. I think Ted was truly amazed that we had succeeded. If I had known the amount of doubt in his mind, I would have never even begun that escapade. Ultimately, Ted worked with the Ringling Bulls as they spent their sunny retirement near Gainesville, Florida. Tragically, Ted died in a Ringling Brother's Circus train wreck. He was with his beloved animals to the end. I will miss you Ted.

# Chapter 11: Bears and Wolves

Every morning at the Wildlife Preserve, someone would make a quick trip to check the caged animals to make sure everything was alright, prior to starting the day feeding and cleaning. This was an important job first thing in the morning. If a lion or something had escaped in the night, you wanted to know it right away. One morning I went up to check on the Bears and Wolves while Ken Parker went to check on the lions. Ken and I shared the senior ranger position at the Wildlife Preserve. We reported directly to the wildlife manager, and were responsible for a staff which numbered eighteen people during the open season.

Ken was the fellow who had been in charge of taking care of the animals that were being held at the animal compound in Clairmont, Florida. He was originally scheduled to work for a proposed park there, but when that park folded and ABC bought the animals, they hired Ken to go up to the Wildlife Preserve. Ken was about the same height as I was, maybe one or two inches taller, and was considerably more trim. Ken was very easy to get along with, and we became friends during the time I spent working down at the compound in Clairmont.

As I pulled my Jeep up over the hill towards the Bear and Wolf section, I had to pass "the mansion" on the hill. This was an old house, built in the 1700's, which stood at the crest of the hill dominating the expanse of the park. From there you could see the whole park, and it was a peaceful place to visit. Surrounding the house were huge old oak trees.

Adjacent to the house was the grave of a child who died in the late 1700's. Rumor has it that the ghost of that child could be seen in the windows of that old mansion on some dark nights. Some of us did think we saw a small figure up in the old mansion windows from time to time but, considering the power of suggestion, I would say this was more likely to have been a child of the mind than a child of the past. Be that as it may, none of us liked to be in that house when the sun was going down.

I pulled down towards the Bear and Wolf holding pen and stopped at the gate. I got out of my Jeep to go unlock the gate and drive into the section. Upon glancing around to check to see if there was anything that might jump on me when I opened the gate, I saw a large black shape in the service area in the middle of the bear holding pens. Even though this particular gate was not supposed to have animals directly behind it, you learn in the animal business to look before something leaps. I realized that the large black shape was one of our black bears and, by the size of it, was either Moses or Gale, two black bears who weighed over 400 pounds. I dropped the unopened lock and chain, turned, jumped back in the Jeep, and hurried off to find Ken so that we could make a plan which would allow us to return the bear to his cage without too much trouble.

I drove down to the lion pen area, and told Ken "Follow me, I have something to show you." We drove back up to the bear and wolf holding pen, hopped out of our Jeeps at the gate, and I pointed to the bear. Ken said something like, "Oh, terrific." We leaned against the Jeep to discuss our plan of attack. We figured we would have to get a little closer look at the pen areas to see how this bear had gotten out. We carefully opened the gate and eased our vehicles inside. We wanted to be able to jump into our Jeeps if that bear decided to go after us. We closed and locked the gate behind us, and walked just far enough to see that someone had left the gate, which opens into the service from one of the pens, open.

I had better give you a description of the pen area, so that you can better follow the next few minutes of the story. The lion pens, the baboon pens, and the bear and wolf pens were all constructed the same way. There were two sets of pens facing each other (Except for the wolves, which had only a single row of pens). These pens were constructed of a poured concrete base, in the shape of a large sledge. These bases were about 18 inches high, and were not attached to the floor. They were set upon a concrete floor in four pairs of two, with four pens in a row.

The tops of the pens were constructed of concrete reinforcing wire. This wire was attached to the sides of the pens with steel strips which were bolted unto the concrete pen bases. This reinforcing wire formed an arch up and over the concrete bases, and was about four feet high at its highest. The ends of the pens faced towards, and away from, the central service area. The ends were also reinforcing wire, but had gates in them to let the animals, or people cleaning the pens, in and out.

The gates were a type known as guillotine gates, because they slid up and down in grooves on either side, and were operated by a pulley and cable system which was attached to the tops of the gates. This system proved to be difficult at times because, not only were the gates heavy and tended to rust, but the reinforcing wire of the pens had four inch square holes. The gate handles would rest right against the wire. This proved to be quite disconcerting if, for instance, a wolf had his muzzle sticking out of the cage to try to bite you when you went to grab the handle.

The outside gates opened unto short sections of alleyways made out of the same wire on top, but the alleyways had wooden floors. These alleyways attached to a run which encircled the pens, so that any animal could be moved into any pen by utilizing the various gates and runs. These runs also opened into the respective display areas, and were the mechanisms used to let the animals out, or allow them to come back into the pens at night. The lion section had an additional holding pen outside the openings to the runs, so that you could get the lions out of the section and into a holding pen without having to run them directly into the cage area. We ended up building a makeshift catch area outside the Bear and Wolf pens as well, but I'll tell you more about that later on.

OK, back to our story. Ken and I decided that we would try to coax the bear back into the open pen ourselves. I told Ken "If we could make sure that the bear was held somehow, I could try to use some bear biscuits to lure it into the cage." Bear biscuits were processed animal food designed to give captive bears a proper diet. We would supplement the bear biscuits from time to time with fruit. However, too much fruit, and the clean up at the bear section was worse that usual. Ken said, "If we could get a rope on him, I could hold him back from the other side of the run, while you try to get him into the cage."

Let me stop here for just a moment to give you a little more insight into the mind of an animal man. Well, into the minds of these two animal men anyway. Ken and I were a lot alike. We made decisions based upon our perceived abilities. The truth is, we probably perceived our abilities to be at a much higher level than they really were. But this was the way we worked, and it kept us alive. During this particular incident, our thoughts were not clouded by any of this "do you think we can do it" business, we simply devised a plan and assumed that it would work.

We went back to the Jeeps and got a lariat. We worked our way down to the pen area. Ken eased around the outside of the runs while I entered the open central service area. You must realize that there was nothing between the bear and myself. I must admit that, although this was a big bear, he had not been too aggressive in the past and I was operating under the assumption that he would probably stay that way. I threw a couple of handfuls of bear biscuits down, right in front of the bear, in an attempt to keep him occupied while we got the rope over him.

I picked up a rake and carefully caught the noose end of the lariat that Ken had draped over the top of the bear run. As I eased that noose over the nose of the bear Ken took up the slack, and we secured the rope around the bear's neck. I saw Ken brace himself with his foot against the bottom of the run directly in front of him. He wrapped the rope around his waist, and leaned back to pull the slack out of the rope.

While all this was happening, the bear was sitting in the middle of the floor munching on bear biscuits. We waited till the bear had finished with his biscuits and, with Ken holding the rope, I started to do the old "follow the trail of bread crumbs" business with the bear biscuits. I would throw a biscuit down just in front of the bear, and get him to move a few inches at a time. As he stood up to get to the first of my strategically placed biscuits, I realized just what a big animal he was. You never really get a feeling for the size of an animal until it is just the animal and you, standing side by side, without any bars or wire between you.

I led this bear towards the open gate in the service area side of his pen. Fortunately, the open gate had been between the bear and myself. If it had been behind the bear, we might have had some additional planning to do. The bear, very calmly, followed me up to the open gate. I placed a bear biscuit on the lip of the entrance to his cage and the bear stuck his head up to get it. As he rocked back to eat that biscuit, I threw a handful of biscuits into the pen. The bear climbed up into the open gate and into the pen.

We had long metal bars which served as locking mechanisms for the guillotine gates. When we closed the gates, we would slide the bars in over the tops of the gates to prevent the gates from being lifted up. We would also slide those bars up underneath the gates when they were open, when we were cleaning, so that the gates would not fall. The bar was in this gate, and as the bear's big butt cleared the gate, I reached over and yanked that bar out and the gate came down with a crash. The bear jumped, turned around, and began pacing angrily, making a slavering growl. I quickly slid the bar back in over the top of the gate to secure it, and stepped back.

Ken threw the rope over to me, and, as the tension eased on the noose around the bear's neck, Moses slid out of it. We recovered the rope, and as Ken swaggered around from the outside of the cage area, I swaggered out from the inside of the cage area. As we walked back to the Jeeps marveling at what great animal men we were, a thought came to me. I asked Ken. "Do you think you could have held that bear if he had gone for me?" Ken stopped and looked down in thought. And as I stopped and turned to face Ken, he raised his head, looked me square in the eye, got a little grin on his face and said. "Now that you mention it, No!" I said. "I didn't think so." We turned. I opened the gate. We hopped in our jeeps and drove off for another thrilling day in the animal business.

We had nine wolves at the Wildlife Preserve, six brown "wolf" colored ones and three black ones. Wolves come in several color types, brown, black, white, etc.. The Wolves were housed, again not surprisingly, in the Bear and Wolf section. The wolves names were Milly, Paw, Madam X, Dopey, Jenny, Jacony, Blackie, Hemorrhoid, and Lobo.

Milly was a beautiful brown female who was very skittish. Paw was a fairly large male, colored almost like a coyote. Madam X was a good looking, nervous, brown female with a small scar under her right eye. Dopey was a pitiful looking brown male at the bottom of the pecking order. Dopey was never any trouble. Jenny was a very nervous brown female. Jacony was a large black male. Blackie was a small black female. Hemorrhoid was a black male. And finally there was Lobo, a very large, brown male who was the leader of the pack.

Putting the wolves up at night was quite interesting. The wolves would consider our efforts some kind of a game, and were smart enough to beat us at it from time to time. They were so much trouble to get back into their cages for the night, that we had to construct an additional catch pen outside the bear and wolf catch cages. This consisted of a wire fence, open on each end where it could be connected to the existing fence. The theory was that if we got the wolves running along the fence line, they would be forced into that holding area and then they could be chased or tempted into the cages more easily. That was how the system was supposed to work, theoretically. We soon found that you could not tempt wolves the way you could the bears.

In reality, we frequently had to resort to other mechanisms which required that we outwit the wolves. No easy task I can tell you. These wolves were some pretty smart cookies. On most occasions the wolves would resist our efforts to put them up for a while, then soon tire of the game, and go in anyway. However, on those select nights, when the wolves were especially frisky, it took ingenuity to get them in, ingenuity and a little daring. I hit upon a technique that worked quite well with a couple of the most difficult wolves to get into the cage.

This technique involved my being out in the wolf section on foot. It was nearly impossible to chase wolves in any given direction, they would simply run some other way, not concerned at all about running right past you. A couple of them weren't too scared of people. As a matter of fact, three of them seemed to want nothing more than to sneak up on you and bite you. A characteristic that would result in the deaths of three wolves, but I'll tell you about that in a minute.

The fact that some of these wolves wanted to sneak up on you, or chase you, lead me to my revolutionary technique. You see, I would turn my back on one wolf at a time, an invitation to the wolf to go for me. As soon as the wolf moved, I would run towards the catch pen. The wolf always accepted the invitation, and came after me with a gleam in his eye. I would run until the wolf was almost on me, then turn very quickly and stop the wolf just before he bit me. This seems like a crazy game, and I suppose it was. I did, however, get the wolves to go in the direction I wanted them to go.

I would play this game until the wolf chased me into the catch cage, then someone would close the fence behind the wolf. We would then have the wolf in a much smaller area where we could maneuver it much more easily. Yes, from time to time my timing was a little off, and I let the wolf get too close before making my turn. They are very quick animals. On these occasions I really appreciated the cut of our pants, which had lots of material near the bottoms of the pants legs. The wolves would bite at me and only catch the cuff of my pants, not my ankles. Most of my uniform pants had the back of their cuffs bitten off.

The tendency to bite existed in only three of our wolves, two brown ones and one black one. The two brown ones were the only ones who would respond to my capture game. The black one, Hemorrhoid, never did chase me. He would always wait for some unsuspecting moment and sneak up on someone. As I have said, this tendency cost the lives of three of the wolves.

There were electric cattle guards at the entrance and exit to the Bear and Wolf section which did not do the kind of job in keeping the animals secure that we had hoped they would. Consequently, we had to station gate guards at the gates. These guards were instructed not to interact with the animals. They were to attempt to chase the animals away from the gate and, failing this, shut the gate. Well, people are even more hard-headed than animals (except maybe for George) so, ultimately, one of the gate guards let the wolf named Hemorrhoid get too close to him, and he got bitten. We called the wolf Hemorrhoid because he was such a pain in the you know where.

The bite was not a bad one, but it did break the skin. After having checked out proper procedures, we reported the bite to all the appropriate agencies. A fellow from one of these agencies came out and said we would have to euthanize (kill) the wolf responsible, and send its head off to be tested for rabies. All of us in the animal business accepted the possibility that we might have to take the series of rabies shots, and the gate guard volunteered to take the shots (I have had them myself and they aren't given with this foot long needle which is stuck into your stomach. They are simply a series of shots you get, like any other, in the deltoid muscle of the upper arm. They are no worse than a tetanus shot.)

We offered to do anything it took to prevent the death of this wolf. We told them that biting was part of his nature and that it was not a sign of rabies. We offered to quarantine Hemorrhoid for as long as it took. The agency representative would have nothing of it. He demanded that the wolf be killed. When he went up to see which wolf had done the deed, the gate guard could not make a "positive identification." The three black wolves we had looked very much alike. We told him it had to be Hemorrhoid, but he didn't care. We told him all we knew about the behaviors of these three wolves, but it didn't matter to him. He then demanded that all three of the black wolves be sacrificed.

We were incensed. We did everything short of beating this guy up, (A thought which had crossed several of our minds), to get him to change his mind, but to no avail. The agency man demanded that we kill these three wolves, and send their heads off for rabies testing. So, under orders from a governmental agency, we euthanized our three black wolves with lethal injection. We sent the heads off to the state laboratory and, of course, the results were negative. No rabies.

Most of the time in the animal business, if something goes wrong you can work to either right the wrong, or prevent that sort of thing from happening again. If we can remain in control, we can do our jobs and fix the problem. But sometimes, control is wrested from our hands and we find ourselves at the mercy of a system which does not just have a mind of its own, it is, in fact, mindless. The feeling of helplessness that one feels when "the system" takes over and destroys the work you have spent your sweat and blood on, is one that burns a permanent scar in your psyche. These wolves lost their lives because of a human being's inability to think. All he knew was to follow orders set up by someone else. The ability to think is supposed to be the difference between man and animals. In this case, man became less than the animals.

# Chapter 12: Baboons

Once upon a time, at the Wildlife Preserve, someone designed a Rhino/Baboon section. It was designed to contain, not surprisingly, Rhinoceroses and Baboons. The design was developed, after many long hours of debate and discussion by many expert animal men.

It was decided that the openings for the gates would have electric cattle guards to keep the Rhinos and Baboons from running out through the gates. It was also decided that the chain-link fence would have an overhang made of chain-link, at an angle of 45 degrees to the fence, pointing into the section. Hanging from the end of this over-hang, would be a two foot section of stiff sheet plastic. The plastic was there so that if the baboons climbed the fence, they couldn't reach up past the hanging plastic sheet to get hold of anything and climb out and, consequently, would be contained inside the Rhino/Baboon area.

Since I have started with "Once upon a time" you should realize that this must be a fairy tale. The thought of keeping the Rhinos and Baboons in with the set-up that we built was just that, no more that a fairy tale.

We had originally ordered 100 Olive baboons from Ethiopia. Thank goodness we never got all 100 of them. The fifty we finally ended up with were more that enough. Olive baboons are relatively large baboons, the males can get up to 80-90 pounds. We housed the baboons in cages which were built for larger animals, and consequently, we had to put additional fencing over them to keep the smaller baboons in. We had fifty baboons in eight cages and the runs and chutes which connected them. I remember the day we let the baboons out in the section we had spent so much time building for them.

Let me go back for just a minute and give you a better idea of the design and construction of this baboon holding area. As I said, the perimeter of the area was chain link fence, this fence was eight feet high. Attached to the top of this fence was another two feet of chain-link fence, which rested upon supports which jutted out from the posts at a 45 degree angle, in towards the section. We were instructed that we needed to attach a two-foot wide plastic sheeting, hanging from the end of the overhang.

We attached this plastic with metal strips we cut out of galvanized strapping material. We took these six inch by three-quarter inch strips and drilled two holes in them, one in either end of the strip, about a quarter of an inch from either end. Drilling the holes was exciting in itself, because if the drill bit got stuck in the metal, the strip would become a rotating buzz saw until you had sense enough to take your finger off the drill trigger.

The metal strips were bent double, and hung from the chain-link overhang. The strips were then fastened to the plastic sheet using pop rivets. Pop rivets are these aluminum fasteners which are designed to go through holes in things, then, when you pull the handle of the pop riveter, a shaft gets pulled through the middle of the pop rivet, and this makes the loose end swell up, so that it won't come out of the hole. The side of the pop rivet next to the pop riveter has a small back plate to prevent it from going through the hole from the other side. When properly aligned and manipulated, the pop rivet serves to hold things together quite well.

They hold things together quite well as long as you have done everything just so. We, on the other hand, were standing on the tops of ladders working eight feet off the ground. We were trying to hold long sheets of plastic in place while bending small metal strips so that the holes would line up, placing the pop rivets in the pop riveter correctly, inserting the pop rivets straightly and, finally, pulling the handle of the pop riveter while keeping the pop rivet straight.

We ended up working at about thirty-three percent efficiency. For every pop rivet we got in, we messed up two. And when you only get the pop rivet in one side of the metal strip, you had to get it out with pliers before you could use that strip again. This frequently made the hole too big so that we had to discard the strip anyway.

I have kept one of those metal strips all these years, as a reminder of just how difficult it was to put that quarter of a mile of plastic sheeting up. I vividly remember the aching arms, the cut up hands, and the frustration which resulted from the construction of that special fence. And the worst part of the whole affair was that, after all that hard work, days and days, the darn fence didn't even keep the baboons in.

So, with that in mind, let's go back to the day we let the baboons out. These baboons had been caught in the wild. They had then been put in crates and had been in those crates since their captivity. When we received the baboons, we immediately put them in the baboon cages, but they were still in cages, albeit big ones. When we first let the baboons out they were ecstatic. They ran and played. They ran up to the small pond we had built and drank. They ate grass and bugs. They simply had a ball.

We had planned that, as we did with the elephants, rhinos, hyenas, lions, bears, and wolves, we would train the baboons to get used to being fed in their cages, so they would go back into the cages for the night. We did this for the protection of the animals, and to make sure that they would not get into anything they shouldn't get into at night. (Remember George.) This technique worked quite well for the elephants (well, most of them), rhinos, lions, and bears. At the end of the day these animals were ready to go "night-night." The wolves were too full of mischief to do anything so routine. The hyenas were just waking up at the end of the day for their natural nighttime life, and the baboons, Oh! the baboons. The baboons were going to have none of it.

After a number of attempts at getting the baboons back into the catch cage, and with dark approaching we gave up. We trusted in our magnificently designed and constructed baboon-proof fence to keep the baboons in and safe. Here we are, back to the fairy tale once again. When we came in to work the next morning, we rushed down to the baboon section and, sure enough, the baboons were gone.

We found them, after much frantic searching, in a wooded area adjacent to the park. It seemed the baboons liked that area very well, and lived in it most of the time they were at the Wildlife Preserve. We never did succeed in keeping them in the section. Oh, we fed them in the section, and tried to get them back into the cages, but were unsuccessful until, after closing the park for the season, we were able to concentrate our efforts in getting them back.

As I said, once we were able to concentrate our efforts, we were able to recapture all fifty of these wayward baboons. I remember the last baboon out. He was a large male, and smart as a whip. He just wouldn't fall for being baited up into the catch cage. We finally ended up having to tranquilize him and carry him back to the cages.

The other residents of the Rhino/Baboon section were, naturally, Rhinos. They stayed in the section about as well as the baboons did. After we found out that the electric cattle guards didn't work on Rhinos, I was instructed to keep an eye on the gates and not let the Rhinos out. Right! I found out that the electric cattle guards didn't work on Rhinos when, one day after having been shocked on the nose once or twice, one of our Rhinos whose name was Bob, decided to just try to walk across it.

Our four white Rhinos were named Bob and Carol and Ted and Alice. (Bob and Carol got moved to Silver Springs, and had their names changed to Andy and Fran, but that's another chapter.) Bob was the largest male, weighing in at about four thousand pounds. That day, Bob started out on this electric cattle guard and stopped about half way. As I watched, Bob just stood there. You could see him jerk as the current pulsed through the cattle guard and his body.

It turned out Bob liked this pretty well. Over the course of the next few days, I would see him intentionally walk out onto the cattle guard, just stand there, and jerk. I don't know what kind of a thrill he was getting, but he sure did seem to like it. Eventually, Bob, Carol, Ted, and Alice simply crossed over into the elephant section and stayed there.

After the rhinos showed a lot more desire to live in the elephant section, and the baboons showed a desire to live anywhere but where they were supposed to, we just gave up. We left the rhinos in the elephant section during the day (Remember, I was out on foot in that section with my elephants and the hyenas, so here were four more things I had to look out for.). We did put the rhinos up as usual during the night.

In the animal business, you have many occasions when you have to give the animals a series of medical treatments. This can manifest itself as a series of injections, or the need to take blood for analysis, or testing the animals for some disease like tuberculosis. Prior to our releasing the baboons, they all had to be tested for tuberculosis, and had to have blood taken from them for some other tests mandated by the government. This meant that each baboon would have to be caught, tested, and have blood taken. Accurate records had to be kept relative to which sample was which, and from which baboon the sample came.

When it was decided that we would test the baboons, our vet Mitch Bush planned for a full day of testing. He came out one fine warm morning and, prior to going down to the baboon section, we tested and bled about thirty fallow deer we had in the holding areas of the main animal barn. Testing fallow deer involves catching them by hand, taking blood from their jugular vein, and TB testing them in the tail fold.

We caught the animals by running them along a fence line. You stand near the fence and, as the deer go between you and the fence, you reach around in front of their neck with one arm, usually your weakest. As the animal's momentum turns you, you grab it up under the belly with the other arm. Once you have the animal stopped, you have to switch the arm from under the animal's neck to over the animal's neck, or the darn thing will butt you in the head.

This is bad enough with animals without horns, (Their heads are even harder that the heads of animal people.) but for those animals with horns, it can be downright disasterous. You could get cut open, or have an eye poked out, or something. It took us about an hour and a half to do these deer, and we were already pretty worn out, sweaty, and dirty, when we headed on down to the baboon section.

We got down to the baboon section, and stood around planning our attack. It was decided that we would get all the baboons out of two of the cages. Then we would run one or two baboons into one of the empty cages, treat them, and put them in the other empty cage until we were finished and able to let them all have the free run of all the cages again. It was critical that we be able to keep track of the individuals we were treating, and these fifty baboons sure did look a lot alike.

It was decided that Dr. Bush would stand just outside the gate in the service area of the baboon pen, assisted by Beth Teeple, the veterinary technician, who would be responsible for preparation and record keeping. Ken Parker would help Dr. Bush control the animals. Someone would go into the cage and wait till the baboons were let into the cage with them. They would then grab the baboon, secure it, and hold it out through the gate until Dr. Bush and Beth were finished. Then they would bring the baboon back in and let it go back into the other empty cage.

There were four of us, Dr. Bush, Beth Teeple, Ken Parker, and myself. And since Dr. Bush, Beth, and Ken all had jobs to do, guess who got to go into the cage and hand capture the baboons? Right, little old me. Actually, it wasn't like I was forced into this job, I wanted to do it. I was a wild and crazy guy, who had the reputation of doing danger-ous things. I really enjoyed the challenge of "me versus an animal." I enjoyed it, that is, when I had a fairly good chance of success. I wouldn't challenge a lion or anything. I wasn't stupid, just cocky .

Well, I proceeded to "don my armor." I wrapped towels around my arms and around my head (To cover my ears, easy targets for baboons), and put on heavy leather gloves. Remember, these were baboons, some of which were half as big as I was. They had big teeth, and wouldn't hesitate to use them. And, as if the teeth weren't bad enough, they had four "hands," so they could really hang on when they wanted to.

The tests we were to do on these baboons required taking blood from the jugular vein, and then doing a Tuberculosis test. The Tuberculosis test consisted of injecting a small amount of tuberculin antigen just under the skin, and then checking for a reaction later. So that we could easily see if there was a response without having to catch the baboons all over again and feel for the "bump", we gave the injec-tion in the eyelid. Now don't get all upset, it was a little bitty injection, and this is the common method for testing primates.

If a baboon came up positive on this test, the eyelid would swell slightly, and we could simply look at the baboon to see if it had a reaction. This method of administration did, however, require that we keep the baboon very still while giving it the injection. However, the last thing the baboons wanted to do was to be still, especially with people grabbing them and doing strange things to them.

Finally, we were ready. I climbed into the cage and, with the ques-tioning looks of my friends and coworkers behind me, instructed them to "Bring 'em on!" As they let the first baboons in the cage with me, I had second thoughts about my decision. I felt like I was in a popcorn maker with baboon sized popcorn with arms and legs, and teeth! I succeeded in grabbing one of the baboons by the arm and, as he concentrated on trying to bite his way through my glove, I secured his arms behind his back and held him out from me. You can handle a monkey quite well this way, it is getting him in that position that can be difficult.

I would hold the baboon out through the gate which was opened after the capture, and Ken would help control the animal while Dr. Bush and Beth administered the treatment. We went on quite successfully for about two hours. When we got down near the end of the troop of baboons, the only ones left were the large males. There were three large males, two slightly smaller than the big boss, but good size never-the-less. They were the hardest to move and, consequently, were the last to get chased into the cage.

I was pretty tired already from the thirty fallow deer and the forty seven baboons we had already done, but we had only three more to do. They let the first one in. I had somewhat more difficulty catching him, then was surprised by his strength. He fought me more than the others had, and it took a great deal of force to keep his arms behind his back and his teeth away from me. We finally finished with him and his other buddy, and had the large dominant male left to do.

I took a short breather then said, "Let's do it." When they let the big boss into the cage, he ran around the cage nervously, just like all the others had done. After a couple of minutes of that, and my failed efforts at catching him, he stopped and turned to face me. I though "Oh great, he wants to fight." He thought about fighting for a couple of seconds but, to my delight, went back to running around the cage.

As he passed me on the left, I grabbed his left arm with my left hand. His weight was great enough that it spun me around quite a bit. As he went to bite me, I grabbed his right arm with my right hand and pulled both arms behind him with all my might, to get them behind his back. He was so large and strong that it took everything I had to secure him. It wasn't bad enough that I was holding on for dear life, he had to keep grabbing the cage with his feet every chance he got.

I finally worked my way to the now open gate, and told my cohorts that they better hurry with this one, because I didn't know how long I could hold him. They finished quickly. I brought the baboon back into the cage and released him as I heard the gate shut behind me. He just stood there for a moment looking at me and trying to figure out just what he had done to deserve this kind of treatment.

After bleeding and Tuberculosis testing eighty animals before one o'clock in the afternoon, we went back up to the veterinary clinic for a much needed rest. The testing of these animals may seem barbaric at times, but please understand that it is necessary for the health of the animals. At the Wildlife Preserve, thanks to the efforts of Dr. Bush and Beth Teeple, we had the healthiest, most productive, group of animals I have ever dealt with. The animals all looked good, and reproduced well in captivity. The long term health of the animals was our primary goal, and we were all dedicated to that goal.

# Chapter 13: Wildlife Preserve Hoofstock

The main animal barn at the wildlife preserve was a thing to behold. It was a large rectangular barn, built with a work area in the shape of an H, inside it. The H described an area where the employees could service the stalls. The stalls were lined up in two rows, one row on either side of the barn. Each stall, or pair of stalls, had its own outside fenced-in run.

The inner stall partitions were removable tongue-in-groove boards, so that the stall sizes could be varied. The sliding gates to the outside runs were operated by a series of ropes and pulleys from inside the barn. The stall doors were massive affairs. They were two inch thick, solid wood, made of diagonal tongue and groove boards, and fastened to the uprights of the barn with three huge hinges. The gates had large metal latches which slid into lockable plates on the frame of the stall.

The H shape was because, inside both ends of the barn, and down six feet from the service areas, were two large bays. These bays had wooden railings up another eight feet, making the height of these bay stalls fourteen feet. The bays were actually much higher than that, because the barn roof was over twenty feet from the bay floor. One bay had big wooden gates, so that rhinos or elephants could be held in it. The other bay had a twelve foot chain link fence across its opening. This bay was used for holding giraffes. That chain link fence did come to give me some trouble one day, however.

One morning when I went up to check on the animals in the barn, I peeked into the giraffe bay and noticed that one of the giraffes looked like it was chewing on the chain link fence. As I got a little closer, I realized that this giraffe had gotten its lower jaw through one of the links in the chain link fence, and was now stuck in the fence. The giraffe had been there for some time now, because there was a stream of saliva running down the fence and unto the floor. I knew I had to do something, because if the giraffe panicked, or slipped, it would probably break its neck.

One of the problems I could see right off, was that this particular giraffe was one of the more nervous of the giraffes. I worried that any attempt to help her might just scare her. I knew I had to cut her out of that fence, and do so quickly before she panicked as the day's work began around the animal barn. I got a pair of side-cutter pliers out of the tool box in the middle of the barn, and eased my way up to the giraffe pen from the top service area. There was a door cut into the wooden fence that surrounded the inside of the bays, through which we used to pass hay and feed for the barn. I opened that door slowly, and was within four feet of the giraffe.

I had to hang out of the door, hold on with my right hand, and try to cut the chain-link from this giraffe's lower jaw with my left hand as I hung out over the bay. When we built the barn, we built it well. The chain link that we used was six gauge. For those of you who know a little about wire, you know that is pretty thick for chain link. So, not only did I have to cut six gauge wire with a little pair of side-cutters, but I had to do it with my left hand (I am right handed), hanging by my right hand from a fence, suspended eight feet in the air.

If all of that wasn't enough, I had to make at least two cuts just to get her free, and I didn't know if she was going to let me make one without panicking. Finally, I eased up to her with my outstretched arm, and slowly brought the pliers up near her jaw. I was talking very calmly and quietly to her as I worked, in an attempt to keep her calm. I told her exactly what I was about to do, and how I was going to do it. I know she didn't understand me, but it's the thought that counts, right?

I worked the pliers around a strand of chain link, and, as I worked to cut through the wire, I watched the giraffe for any signs of panic. Fortunately for both of us, she seemed to realize that I was there to help, and stood very still. It would always amaze me when a formerly unmanageable animal would remain very calm under crisis situations, as if it knew you were there to help it.

I made it through one strand of wire, and let my arm fall to my side for a short rest. After just a moment, I went back to the next strand I had chosen and, with somewhat more trouble because my hand was tiring. I cut through it. I thought this cut would release her, but it didn't. It turned out that I had to make one more cut. I went back to work and, with gritted teeth, succeeded in cutting a third strand. As this strand snapped, the tension on the giraffe's jaw was released and she backed free. She moved her jaw around and licked her lips a few times, but she seemed to be none the worse for wear and had no adverse effects from her ordeal. I swung myself up into the service area of the barn, and wondered what other adventures awaited me this fine bright morning.

One day, a famous brewery group was visiting the Washington D. C. area, and needed a place to house their Clydesdale horses. We had this large animal barn, specially designed to handle large animals, and the management thought the PR would be good for us, so we offered our quarters for their horses. They arrived in this huge animal hauling truck, and their handlers unloaded them out by the road. These animals are huge, over six feet tall, and about a ton apiece. Their horseshoes are a foot across.

The handlers walked these very calm animals up and into the barn. The stalls had been previously prepared. We had cleaned them especially well, and had laid fresh bedding down in each stall. As the handlers brought the horses in, the horses would be put into individual stalls where food and water waited for them.

All went quite well until the next to the last horse was put in the barn. This particular horse didn't show any signs of nervousness. He appeared as calm as all the other ones had been. However, inside his head, he must have had other thoughts. As the groom walked this big horse into the stall, everything seemed normal. The groom turned the horse loose, and closed the stall door behind him. He set the latch in the door, and walked back to get the last horse. As he turned, there came a blast as if dynamite had gone off inside one of the stalls.

As we reacted to the noise, we saw the next to the last stall door fly off and hit the opposite wall with a crash. As I have said, these doors were designed to hold some pretty big animals. Remember, they were solid oak, and had three massive hinges on one side. The latch was steel, and bolted to the framework of the door. But, regardless of the construction of this door, that Clydesdale had blasted it off its hinges with one kick from those huge back legs. If the groom had still been standing outside that door, it probably would have crushed him.

We walked back over to the stall, peeked in, and there was the horse, calmly munching some food. It seems he was simply making a statement about the facilities. The door was lying askew up against the bay wall, and had four big holes in it where the cleats from the horse's shoes had hit it. We carefully went to work remounting the door, but had no other trouble with this horse. They put the last horse in the last stall, and everyone settled down for the night. I guess that sometimes an animal just has to express itself the only way it can.

Speaking of self expression, let me introduce you to Go-Goat. It was just another day at work. We had moved a nanny goat up from cuddle corner to the main animal barn because she was about due to have kids. She was part African pygmy goat, those are the ones you always see in the contact areas (petting zoo) of big zoos and fairs. They are the little black and white ones with the big bellies. I always thought they were quite attractive, as goats go. She had been bred by a full blooded pygmy buck. We had goats born all the time around there, so nothing special was planned.

The following morning, when we entered the main animal barn to make our morning rounds, we found a newborn baby goat, semi-conscious, lying on the concrete floor of the service area outside the nanny's pen. We took the little female kid to the Vet clinic, put it on a heating pad, and watched it carefully until it revived somewhat. It seems as though it had rolled out under the door of the stall where we had put its mother, after it was born.

We attempted to give the baby back to its mother but she would have nothing to do with it. We milked the mother to get the baby some necessary colostrum milk. The first milk mothers produce is full of antibodies necessary for the babies, so that they can develop a fully functional immune system, and to "jump start" the baby's digestive system. I have milked some pretty strange things in my life. You don't even need a milking stool for giraffes!

Well, we realized that we had another baby someone had to bottle raise at home for a while. This kind of thing happened on a fairly regular basis. I volunteered. I took the baby goat home, to the delight of my 60 pound female collie/terrier mutt. I had trouble at first, as you often do, trying to get the baby to take to a bottle. This process wasn't helped much by the fact that the goat wanted to nurse off the dog, and the dog seemed quite content to let it try. It would have been fine if the dog had had milk, but she had never even had puppies before, and was never ever going to have them in the future, if you know what I mean.

I bottle-fed the goat with a specially prepared milk substitute, and I eventually got her to eat. However, when it was time to wean the goat and get her to eat solid food, I ran into a snag. Usually, you can get an animal started eating solid food by introducing some of the solid food, a little at a time, into its milk. This gets the animal used to the taste, and gets it's system ready to handle the change of diet. You gradually increase the solid food to milk ratio, until the animal is weaned.

That is the way it usually works. Not with this goat, though. This goat would refuse milk with even one pellet of solid food in it. You have heard the old stories about goats eating everything, not this one. She wouldn't eat anything but her milk. So I decided that I would have to cold wean this animal. That is when you simply remove the milk, offer the solid food and wait until the animal gets hungry enough to eat it.

This process sounds awfully cruel, but, as the animals age, their system changes to the point where they need solid food. This is especially true of ruminants, like goats and other members of the ruminant family who "chew their cud". As you can guess, this goat was stubborn. She refused to eat for three days. As soon as I would get home, she would come running up, crying, looking for her bottle. By the way, I kept this goat in my house.

She was getting skinny and I was afraid she would get sick, so I gave in and fed her. During that time, the goat was always in the dog's bowl when I fed the dog, trying to figure out what her "mother" was so interested in. I fed the dog Ken-L-Ration Biscuit, and eventually the goat started to eat it. That goat got used to that dog food, and never would eat anything else.

I had been calling the goat "goat" all this time. When I let the goat outside, from time to time, she would take off like a shot and run around in the yard having a great time. It was during one of those sessions that I finally started calling her Go-Goat. The name stuck, and a go goat she was. Go-Goat had her own room in the house. I had trained her to use a cat litter box so I didn't have to clean up the entire room. But she had a nasty habit of eating the walls. She loved to eat wallboard. Her appetite caused me to have to panel her room before I left that house.

Go-goat was something else. She was a notorious hit and run creature. She loved to chew on fabric or paper. If you didn't watch her, she would chew a hole in your clothes. She also had the nasty habit of ripping the bottom out of your grocery bags before you could set them down.

Go-Goat was like any other goat in her desire to jump up on things. She would sit on the couch when I watched TV, and even climb up on the back of the couch. This desire to climb got her in trouble with my mother one day. My mother was visiting and, to keep busy, was out weeding our garden. She was bending over, and apparently her back was too much of a temptation for Go-Goat to stand. The next thing I know, mom gives out a yell. I looked out the window, and there is Go-Goat perched on my mother's back. Mom wasn't hurt, even though Go-Goat weighed about twenty pounds and had those little sharp hooves. However, mom did learn not to turn her back on Go-Goat anymore.

Go-Goat was a pretty tough cookie all the way around. One day Go-Goat and I were outside in the yard when a strange German Shepherd came trotting down the road. When the dog saw Go-Goat, he gave a low "woof," and came running at full speed towards the goat. Go-Goat simply shifted herself so that she was at a slight angle to the onrushing dog. As the dog got closer, Go-Goat cocked her head and bristled up the hair along her spine. I knew what Go-Goat intended for the dog, and I stood back and watched.

Just when the dog got a few feet from Go-Goat, Go-Goat raised up on her hind legs. When the dog was close enough, Go-Goat came down hard with her little horns right on the top of that dog's head. The impact drove the dog down unto the road. That dog got up yelping, and took off back up the road at top speed. Go-Goat couldn't contain her delight. She chased the dog for about thirty feet, then just danced, and jumped her way back to where I was.

Early on in Go-Goat's life I had purchased her from the Wildlife Preserve. I finally gave Go-Goat to one of the guys from the mainte-nance department who had a big farm. Go-Goat needed more room to run, and other animals to relate to. A couple of days after I had given Go-Goat away, the guy I gave her to came in and said that Go-Goat was doing great, but that she had somehow gotten up on the top of his barn. The guy said he had the devil of a time getting her down. I told him that life with Go-Goat was probably going to be an exciting adventure.

Now, let me shift gears, and ask you a few questions. If you were going to open a *wild animal* park, what sorts of things would you need to acquire? Right! wild animals. And where would you get these wild animals? Well, you could get them from the wild, true, but wouldn't it be easier to buy them from somebody that had already captured them and brought them over to this country, and save yourself all that trouble? Sure it would. There is, however, one problem with this scenario.

If you had a bunch of animals, and someone wanted to buy some of them, which ones would you sell him? Would you sell him the prettiest ones, the ones easiest to handle? No you wouldn't! Admit it now! You would sell him the meanest, nastiest, ugliest animals you had, so that you could get rid of these hard-heads, now wouldn't you? Of course you would!

Consequently, the problem with opening a new wild animal park is that you, invariably, get the ugly, hard-headed animals that no one else wants, or can handle. The wonderful thing about my career in the animal business, is that I was involved in creating, and opening, four wild animal parks, that's four times the trouble. (That's why I ended up with George.) Anyway, let me tell you a little about three of these types of characters. Their names were Freight Train, Steamroller, and Demolition. Does this bode well for their dispositions? No, it doesn't!

These three idiots were American bison, big American bison. They were all mean and nasty, and did everything they could to cause trouble. They all weighed in at over 1000 pounds and could, consequently, be a whole lot of trouble. The worst of the bunch, however, was Demolition. He loved nothing more than to harass people and animals. He had been in so many fights that his horns were worn down to nubs. (Kinda reminiscent of Shagnasty. Same disposition.)

Demolition also had this particular dislike for the backhoe. Whenever he would hear the backhoe's engine, he would come running over to fight with it. It didn't matter that the backhoe was several times bigger than he was, he didn't like it. He would charge the backhoe, and run into the tires. Most of the time, however, he just bucked, and jumped, and growled; running around and around it, until he got tired, or until we drove off.

Demolition got his comeuppance one day, however, on the horns of a yak. I really like yaks. They are big and strong, but they are peaceful and just kind of mind their own business. The large male yak we had I called Boromir (from Tolkien's *The Lord of the Rings*). He was a good sized male, weighing about 800 pounds. Yaks are those shaggy black animals from Tibet. They have long horns which are several feet from tip to tip. Domestic yak, which are smaller than wild yak, are used for pack animals and for their wool and milk.

One day, Demolition was being his nasty self, looking for someone to pick on, when Boromir walked by. Demolition started in on him, jumping around, and acting like he was tough. They butted heads a few times, but basically Boromir was ignoring Demolition. This just served to make Demolition madder. Demolition finally came around to the downhill side of Boromir, and got between him and the fence. Boromir saw his chance and wheeled very quickly. He hooked Demolition up under the belly with that wide set of horns.

With one mighty lunge and contraction of his neck muscles, Boromir lifted Demolition off his feet, and threw him through the fence. The fence fabric didn't break, but the fence was knocked flat for about thirty-five feet by the impact. Demolition rolled over a couple of times as he went down the hill. When Demolition stopped rolling, he got up kind of wobbly and took off in the opposite direction.

Meanwhile, Boromir continued on his way, moving easily, minding his own business.

As I have mentioned, and as you well know, sometimes, despite your best laid plans, things can go wrong. One day, at the Wildlife Preserve, one of our fallow deer came up missing. One of the daily tasks in the animal business is to do a morning head count. You always wanted to make sure everything was where it was supposed to be. This particular fallow deer was a large white male and, try as we might, we couldn't find him anywhere. We wondered what had happened to him, and instituted a park-wide search. Still no luck. He was nowhere to be found.

As I have said, the Wildlife Preserve was just to the east of Washington, D. C.. We were located outside the beltway, near Mitchellville, Maryland, approximately eleven miles from downtown Washington. One day, several weeks after losing this fallow deer, we got a call from the Washington police. They said that people had been reporting this strange deer in one of the small parks downtown, and would we like to come check it out. We said we would be glad to, but at the time never connected the sighting with our escaped fallow deer. We didn't even consider the possibility that he had gotten across the Washington beltway, and was living in downtown Washington D. C.

We got to the park to which the police had directed us, but couldn't find anything. Some of the local citizens had gathered as we were making out search, and said they had seen this big white deer running around loose in the park. We looked at each other, kind of shook our heads, and said "Noooo." Well, It turned out to be "Yeeees."

We got several calls after that, over a period of four months. We never did get to a park in time to see the deer, but we knew it had to be a fallow deer by the descriptions we were getting, large white deer with big antlers. We still weren't convinced that it was ours, however, after all, the National Zoo was closer than we were.

One day we got a call that the deer had been sighted in this large park down near the capitol. The police were waiting at the park for us and, consequently, had been able to keep an eye on the deer. When we saw it, we realized, then and there, that it was ours. We loaded up the tranquilizer gun, and stalked this deer to get a shot. This was no easy task. This deer was sharp. Think about it, it would have to be sharp to travel into Washington, D. C. and survive for four months. It also looked very healthy even after all that time.

We darted the animal and waited. No response. Fallow deer are quite resistant to most tranquilizer drugs. We took a chance and darted him again, and got no response. This deer didn't even slow down. We had given him enough dope to stop ten elephants, and he wasn't having any of it. We finally lost him. (It is amazing how sharp animals can be sometimes. But to them it is a life or death struggle, remember.)

We pulled back in defeat. We told the police to keep us informed, that we were sorry we failed, and went on back to the park. We continued to get reports of this deer for about a month, then the reports stopped. We all figured he had finally met some tragic end like being attacked by dogs, or being hit by a car. And, so, it was with total amazement, that about one month later, six months after his disappearance, I looked down the service road, inside the gates of the Wildlife Preserve, and saw this large white deer trotting easily up the road.

I ran down to the holding areas behind the main animal barn and opened the gate. He was moving easily towards the gate, so I just backed off to see what he would do. The gate was not in a corner or anything, and this deer could have chosen to go in any of a dozen different directions, but he didn't. He just trotted up that road as calm as you please and right through the gate into the holding pen. If I hadn't seen it with my own eyes, I wouldn't have believed it.

It seems that this deer had gotten tired of his lonely life in the "wilds" of Washington, D. C., and decided to come on back home where the pickings were easier. He was in great shape, not skinny or scarred. He simply sauntered back into the herd of other fallow deer, like he had only been gone a minute or two.

It is on these occasions that I really appreciate the life force animals carry with them. This animal survived six months in downtown Washington, D.C., crossing the Washington beltway at least twice. He found his way back, over eleven miles of densely populated country, to the park he had left six months before. He survived, even thrived, where some *people* have a hard time living. It is truly a testament to the will to live.

# Chapter 14: Birds

At Silver Springs, we had several members of the parrot family. Many of these parrots were display animals. We would put them out on perches during the day to liven up the Reptile Institute. They are colorful, noisy birds which make a good, easy display. We kept them from flying away by trimming the flight feathers on one wing. These feathers would eventually be replaced, consequently, these birds had to be trimmed regularly. We felt that trimming was much more acceptable that pinioning, or tenectomizing, which required surgery to permanently prevent them from flying. The only problem with just trimming the wings was that, if you misjudged the time when the bird needed to be trimmed, the bird flew away.

As it would happen, one of our macaws did just that. One day, one of our blue and gold macaws left the Reptile Institute. It simply took off and flew off of the Silver Springs property. We made an attempt to follow it, but it soon lost us in the woods across Highway 40. We would get reports of this big, brightly-colored bird across the highway from time to time, but it was usually gone when we got there.

One day I answered the call and, surprisingly enough, the macaw was still there when I got there. I radioed my crew to join me, having decided that we would attempt to capture this wayward bird. It was my intent to try to coax the bird unto a long pole we used to put the birds on their perches. These poles were up to fifteen feet long, and round. The birds were used to climbing unto them since they were moved regularly. I also wanted to keep the bird moving if it refused to get on the pole, in the hopes that it would tire, and get low enough to catch by hand.

After several hours of trying to catch this bird, I realized it might end up as a waiting game. I sent my crew back to take care of the other animals since it was, by now, the end of the day. I also asked them to get me a sandwich and some drinks from food service at Silver Springs, and to tell my boss that I was going to stay with this bird for as long as it took.

I succeeded in moving the bird back on Silver Springs property at about dusk. The bird was flying with effort. Remember, this bird had not been flying for several years. Its latest escapade had probably tired it out, and it may have been quite sore. Think about how you feel after your first few days back at exercising, after you have been making up excuses not to go work out for several months. Hurts doesn't it. I know this syndrome all too well.

I thought I had him as he got lower and lower, but, just as he was going to get close enough for me to make a grab, he made one last Herculean effort. He managed to get enough lift to get up into the lower branches of a cypress tree, some ten feet beyond the reach of my perch pole. He sat down on that branch and, as dusk fell, I saw him close his eyes and fall off to sleep. I wasn't going to take a chance on him moving during the night, so I made the decision to wait him out.

He was in a well lighted part of the park, and I simply sat and watched him all night. Oh, I took one or two breaks when one of our security guards, a super guy and good friend named Floyd, would keep an eye on him for me. During these times I would get some coffee, or get rid of some coffee, but was soon back on my post. Floyd had other duties to take care of, and I couldn't take too much time out of his schedule.

As dawn broke over Silver Springs (This is one of the most beautiful scenes in all of nature, mist rising over the crystal clear water, animals rising in voice to welcome the morning.), the macaw roused. I made an attempt to move him right away. I didn't want to be chasing this bird around with this great long pole, with three or four thousand people asking me what I was doing. His labored flying indicated his lack of condition, and I figured if I just kept on him, I could catch him. You must realize, I wasn't in top form myself. I had just stayed up all night after a hard day's work, and I really looked like it (and smelled like it, I bet). I was wearing a dirty, sweaty uniform, and had a day's growth of beard. I was not very presentable to a park full of guests.

The macaw flew slowly from tree to tree, but I kept on him. Finally, he made a move to cross the river. For a moment I didn't think he would make it, and had nightmares of some alligator getting him before I did. But he gave a last burst of effort and got across. I had to relinquish my visual contact with him so that I could go all the way around the park and come upon him from the animal sections, into which he had flown.

I searched for about thirty minutes before I finally found him. I moved him further away from the river. He was getting lower and lower in the vegetation. He was within reach of the pole now, but would have nothing to do with it. I kept on him till he finally made a failed attempt to achieve enough height to make a branch. As he flew just below it, he ran out of steam and landed on the ground.

I ran over to where he was strutting around among the palmettos, squawking and fussing. I carefully reached down with the pole, but he wouldn't get on it. Using the pole to keep his beak away from me (they can bit the snot out of you if you aren't careful), I reached down and grabbed him. He really regaled me with a vocal tirade, but there was no way I was letting him go now. I carried him back up to the holding pens in the Reptile Institute, clipped his wings, gave him some fruit and

water, and headed on home for a well deserved rest. This time persever-
ance paid off.

Let me take a few minutes to tell you about my least favorite animals
of all, the ostriches. My dislike for ostriches is one cultivated over many
years of having to deal with them. They are big, powerful, potentially
dangerous, animals with a brain about the size of a pea, not all of which
they use at any given moment.

At Lion Country, I have seen times when, during an ice storm,
(those of you familiar with Atlanta can really appreciate what I mean)
the stupid ostriches would sit down, right in the middle of the road,
and literally get frozen to the road by a sheet of ice. Their feathers act as
insulation and the ice covers their entire body. I have had to break the
ice from around the outside of their feathers just so that they could
stand up. They are the classic example of something that doesn't have
enough sense to come in out of the rain.

As I said, they can be very dangerous. They can weigh up to 500
pounds, and they kick forward when they attack. Their foot is modified
so that it only has two toes. One small toe for stabilization and one
great toe, with a large nail in it for defense. They kick forward, and
down, with this great toe, and have been known to disembowel animals
and people who have gotten in their way.

Now, they aren't always looking to stomp on someone, but the problem
is, you never know when they are going to change their mind (I use the
word mind for the want of a better word). You can be walking along,
minding your own business when a ostrich will look over at you as if you
just appeared out of nowhere. It doesn't matter that you have just been
feeding him the moment before. He will look at you and attack.

Their attack is swift and dedicated. They are so stupid that once they
begin the attack, they just continue until they get the message from that
pea brain to stop. That can, in fact, occur right in the middle of a fight.
I have seen them attack and be winning, and right in the middle of

their attack, look as if they had seen a ghost, and run off with wings raised, bobbing and weaving like some punch drunk fighter. I have also seen them attack, only to notice some interesting bit of something, stop, and start trying to eat that thing that caught their eye. These guys are real nutcases!

Of all the interactions I have had with ostriches in my career, two stand out. Once, while I was doing my morning feeding run along the Silver River by boat. (Some of the most glorious times I ever had in the animal business were cruising along that mist-shrouded river early in the morning.) I stopped off to feed the Zebras we had on an island on the Jungle Cruise canal. Some time back we had put this large male ostrich on this island to reduce his contact with people. He was naturally mean, and we could never trust him. Prior to carrying the food up onto the island, I would always look to see if this ostrich was close. If he was, I would move the boat and feed somewhere else. The boat I used was a little V-hulled work boat, all beat up, and propelled by a twenty-five horsepower Johnson motor.

I pulled up into the little cove where I usually stopped, turned the motor off, and stood up to look for this ostrich. The island is heavily treed, with big cypresses and other southern trees, so you had to look around a little bit to make sure this ostrich wasn't too close. I couldn't see him, so I picked up the metal trash can I used to carry the feed for the zebras, and climbed out of the boat.

The trash can was one of those ordinary galvanized garbage cans with the handles on the sides. I walked up to where I was going to feed the zebras and set the bucket down. I went back to the boat to get a few flakes of hay for the zebras, and walked back up to where the trash can was. I put the hay flakes down, dumped the feed on top of them, turned, and headed back to the boat.

Just as I got to the boat, I felt something was about to happen. I don't know whether I heard him coming, or felt some change in the air pressure, or just got the message somehow, but I turned in time to see this big male ostrich right on top of me. As I turned, I still had hold of the trash can, and it was a good thing I did. I turned just as the ostrich got to me, and as I finished my turn, he kicked. His kick hit the trash can hard, and crushed it against my chest. The impact knocked me back into the boat and out of his reach. Oh, he was still there hissing to beat the band, and madder than ever because he couldn't get to me because I was in the bottom of the boat.

When I got control of myself, in that unsteady boat, I climbed to the back of the boat and picked up the trash can that had saved my skin. Ignoring the little cuts and bruises I had gotten when I fell into the boat, I examined the can. It was squashed flat. On the side where the ostrich hit it, there was a hole in the metal the size of a half-dollar. The great toe of that ostrich had penetrated that galvanized trash can as if it were aluminum foil. Since a lot of the force of the kick had been dissipated by the crushing of the can, the side of the can next to me, the inside of the side next to my chest, was only dented. After finishing with my feeding run I got back up to the wildlife office, and we all had a good laugh over my trophy trash can. I can tell you though, it wasn't very funny at the moment it happened.

Another ostrich story that comes to mind is not nearly so exciting, but interesting nevertheless. One day, upon making morning rounds at Silver Springs, I noticed a female ostrich with what looked like a stick stuck in her throat. Everyone has seen the cartoon ostriches and how they eat just about anything, well it's true. If they can get it through their beak, they'll eat it.

It looked as though this ostrich had swallowed a stick for some reason, and it had lodged sideways in her throat. It seemed to be exerting a great deal of pressure on the throat tissues, so I called the vet right away. He came out and was very concerned that if he tried anything, it would simply puncture her throat and we would lose her. I told him that was OK he needn't take that responsibility, I would take care of it. I did most of the veterinary work anyway as a cost-effective strategy.

My assistant, Scott Sutton, and I cornered this ostrich with my Bronco and some plywood, so that she couldn't move around much. I told him that he was to hold her mouth open, and I would try to reach down her throat and see if I could dislodge the stick without doing too much damage to her throat. I know this must seem like a strange and disgusting thing to do, but remember, this is the animal business, it is our job to be strange and disgusting.

I got a tube of K-Y Jelly out of the emergency kit. K-Y Jelly is a lubricant doctors and veterinarians use because, unlike Vaseline, it washes off easily. I took the K-Y Jelly and greased up my right arm, all the way to the arm pit. We grabbed the ostrich's head and, while I held the bottom jaw, Scott held her head still, and held the top jaw open. I slid my arm down her esophagus, and quickly encountered some packed food. This ostrich had continued to eat, even though the food wasn't moving down her throat. I knew that I had to limit the time my arm was in her esophagus, because the size of my arm constricted her trachea, and she couldn't breathe when my arm was in her throat. You could tell she knew this too, because she really didn't like what we were doing to her.

I pulled up a hand full of already swallowed feed, and went back for another grope. This feed had already started to ferment in that warm slimy environment, and, consequently, didn't smell too good. But we were committed. (Lots of people said we should be committed, so I guess we were simply following instructions.) After pulling out another handful of feed, I could finally feel what she had swallowed.

Stuck sideways in this ostrich's throat was the broken remains of half an ostrich eggshell. Now, ostriches frequently eat broken eggshells, but they usually break them into smaller pieces. The females eat egg shells as a mechanism for retrieving some of the calcium they use in producing those giant eggs. When I realized what it was, I turned it over with my fingertips, so that the curved side was up, and pulled it out. We turned the ostrich loose, and, after a few shakes of her head, she went right to eating again, she never showed any adverse signs of her somewhat strange ordeal. I, on the other hand, needed a little soap and water, but that's all in a day's work.

A sarus crane is a large gray bird with a red head. The head is not all red, because there is a round patch of white or light gray on top of the head, as if they were balding. These cranes are the largest members of the crane family, standing five feet tall. They have a wing span of about seven feet. They are native to India. We purchased a pair of sarus cranes for the Jungle Cruise display at Silver Springs. We placed them on the point of land where the zebras were (The same place we put that mean male ostrich I told you about).

Our hopes were that these two animals would feel secure enough to breed in captivity. This is the primary goal that I maintained the entire time I was in the animal business. I felt that if the animals successfully reproduced, they must be getting the kind of care they need. Our hopes were soon realized when we noticed breeding activity and, not long after that, nest building behavior.

The nests these animals build are massive affairs, four feet in diameter, constructed right on the ground. They use sticks of all sizes, from six inches long to two feet long. There are no materials used to "soften" the center of the nests. The first two eggs were laid, one day apart. We waited anxiously as the cranes incubated the eggs. We would walk up to the nest each day to check on things, but were repelled by one or both of the cranes, who would stand at their full height, with wings outspread, and hiss. They would attempt to spear you if you got too close. They had the weapon for it too, eight inches of pointed beak.

In about one month the first egg hatched. These cranes, as do many large birds, lay two eggs, one day apart, which hatch one day apart. The second chick frequently dies, so these birds usually only raise one young. A day after the first chick hatched, the other chick hatched. Sarus crane chicks are known as precocious. That means they are up and ready to go just hours after they are hatched, as opposed to those chicks who have to stay in the nest for a long time and develop.

As soon as the second chick was mobile, all four of the cranes were off the nest and wandering around the section. We didn't worry too much about the chicks. We were having so much trouble checking on them, because the adults were so aggressive, we didn't figure anything could get close. We were wrong.

The next morning the chicks were gone. We searched every inch of that point, but couldn't find a trace of them. We figured that some animal had gotten them in the night. There were raccoons, opossums, turtles, alligators, hawks, owls, even monkeys, which had access to the area.

We were very disturbed, and vowed to catch the young next year and put them in a predator-proof pen we would build up near the wildlife office. After we had all but forgotten about the loss of the baby cranes, we found another egg in the same nest. The next day, there were two eggs in the nest and the female was sitting on them.

What we didn't know at the time, but what is well know now, was that many of these large birds will lay another series of eggs if the chicks die soon after hatching or something happens to the first clutch of eggs. This factor has helped to lead to the reintroduction of the California Condor to the wild. The zoos which are breeding the condors are pulling the eggs soon after they are laid and incubating them. The adult pairs are then laying more eggs. In this fashion, you can get twice the normal production of young.

We got to work on our predator-proof pen, and waited for the arrival of the second set of chicks, determined not to let these chicks die. As soon as the first chick hatched, almost everyone wanted to pull the birds then. What if the second egg didn't hatch? What if something got the chick that night? But I convinced them to wait. I don't know why, but I knew the parents would protect that one chick until the other one hatched.

Sure enough, the next morning there were two chicks, and they were up and walking around the section. It proved to be much easier to catch these animals than I had thought it might be. The parents were so protective of their babies that they stood their ground and didn't run away. The babies were simply following those four long legs attached to their parents high above.

We set about to catch the four cranes and move them to the holding pen. In an attempt to protect their young, the sarus canes would lunge at us with those long pointed beaks to try to skewer us, but this was their undoing. When they lunged, if you were fast enough, you could grab the beak before they had time to pull it back for another stab. Like I said, you could grab the beak if you were fast enough. If you weren't, you usually got a hole in your hand for the effort.

After you grabbed their beak, you had to pull the bird in close to you, fold those seven foot wings in, and get control of those long legs, legs ending in three toes equipped with claws. You had to fold the bird up like this for two reasons. First, we had to make sure that we didn't injure the bird. Second, we had to make sure that the bird didn't injure us. After catching the adults, it was simply a matter of picking up the now confused chicks. All in all, the move went very well.

We carried the birds up to the new holding pen we had made and let the chicks grow up. The pen had been carefully designed to prevent any ground dwelling predator as well as any predatory bird from getting at the chicks. When we felt the chicks were large enough to take care of themselves, we took them all back down to the section and released them. What we didn't know at the time, was that that section was big enough for one pair of birds, but not big enough for two pairs of birds. We soon found this out.

Every year, like clockwork, the sarus cranes would raise two babies. They got so prolific that we had to start selling them, or trading them for other animals. That was OK with me though, I never did get enough money to satisfy my animal acquisition needs. Anyway, there is still one story I want to tell you about the first set of young sarus cranes and the space requirements of sarus cranes.

One morning, as I made my morning feeding run, I noticed that the two younger birds from the very first clutch were not on the point. The babies had grown to be the same size as their parents by now, but did not quite have their full adult coloration. I spotted the young birds on the opposite side of the canal. One of them was in the Giraffe section and one of them was in the Rhino section. They seemed to be doing fine, so I finished my run and went back up to get the crew to move them back to the point.

We chased the birds back onto the point fairly easily, chasing the birds into the canal, and swam them across the canal and back onto the point. They swim quite well, high up out of the water. However, as time went on, we would find them off the point more and more frequently. We didn't know at the time, that there just wasn't enough psychological room for four birds on that point.

On one occasion, one of the birds did not move easily. Instead of crossing the canal back to the point, he made a break for the cypress lowlands which line the Silver River. We took off in hot pursuit. Running through a cypress swamp is a wonderfully engrossing experience. The main goal of the chase was, of course, to catch the bird. There were other secondary goals, however, like self-preservation.

As one runs through the cypress trees, trying to maintain one's footing in the black ooze of centuries of decay, one is constantly reminded of the existence of that phenomenon know as the cypress "knee." These are woody protuberances sticking up from the roots of the cypress tree at random intervals. They can be like small bumps at ground level, or stand as high as your head However, I can tell you from experience, most of them are just about shin high. It isn't bad enough that you are constantly banging *your* knees on *their* "knees", if you trip over one, chances are you are going to land on two or three more of them. A very unpleasant occurrence, made even more unpleasant if some favorite part of your anatomy is the target of one of these cypress "knees."

If the muck and the cypress "knees" weren't bad enough, mother nature put an added bit of excitement into this scene, Golden Orb Spiders. First of all, I must tell you that, of all the animals I have worked, none of them scares me like spiders do. They are my one great fear, well, one of my several great fears. I would rather go into a lion cage than to have to interact with a spider. I want you to remember this as I describe this next bit.

These Golden Orb Spiders can get quite large, five to six inches across the span of their legs. They build their large webs between the trees and bushes in the swamp. They live all over down here in Florida, but we are in the swamp, remember. The silk they spin is golden colored, hence the name Golden Orb Spider. Well, on with the chase.

As you run through the cypress swamp, making sure you don't slip in the mud, or trip over a cypress "knee" and impale yourself, while trying to watch a bird so that it doesn't get away from you, the last thing you need is another distraction. But sometimes you are concentrating so hard on your task that you forget about the Golden Orb Spiders. Yes, even I forgot about The Golden Orb Spiders from time to time. As a matter of fact, I try not to think about spiders at all.

As fate would have it, these spiders build their webs just about face high to me. Are you getting ahead of me? As we ran through the swamp, I ducked under a branch and, still moving full speed, straightened back up and right smack into the center of one of these big spider's webs. My momentum carried me past the spot where it was built, and it came loose from its supports. Now, let me paint you a picture of the scene.

It was cool and dark up under those cypress trees, the river gurgling softly behind me, a sarus crane running frantically away from this creature (me) who had erupted from under a bush. I had come up into that spider web, and it had released itself from its supports and had molded itself to my head. If the web wasn't enough to give me the heebie-jeebies, and it was, here I was, face to spider, with what was perhaps the largest spider in the whole wide world. At least it seemed that way at the time.

These spiders spin their webs, then sit right in the middle of the web, waiting for some unsuspecting bug to come along and get caught. This spider got more than it had bargained for. Fortunately for me, the spider had been on the other side of the web, or I would have been caught inside that web, with the spider inside of its own web with me. I have been bitten by one of these spiders, and I still carry a scar up under my arm from the abscess the venom induced. But inside or out, this was a nightmare come true for me.

I screamed and pawed at my face like a madman. I think I must have knocked the spider off with the first swing, but I didn't stop until all of that enveloping web was off of me. I even had it in my mouth, where I had opened my mouth to scream. I was stomping up and down at the same time, and must have been quite a sight.

After I got the web off, and quieted the goose flesh somewhat, I remembered I had a crane to catch. Still shivering from my spider encounter, I took up the chase once again. I chased the bird down to the river and thought I could catch it when it entered the water. The crane jumped in the water and started to swim across the Silver River, floating easily on top of the water. I jumped in the river not too long after it did. I had forgotten that the water at this spot was over my head. I sank like a stone.

Kicking wildly with my new, heavy, work boots, I only succeeded in pulling myself deeper in the water. Panic overcame me once again, and I just knew I was going to die. It hadn't been bad enough that I had gotten a spider plastered to my face, but now I was going to drown myself chasing a bird. I could see the headlines, "Wildlife expert drowns chasing bird."

I quickly got control of my fear and relaxed. This is a quality you have to have in the animal business, or you are going to suffer a lot more than usual. I slowly swam to the surface, using only my arms, and took a glorious breath of air. I felt I could make it across the river, swimming with just my arms, so I headed out after the bird again who, by now, was over halfway across.

After getting about half way across myself, I though that this was one more of those snap decisions I should have taken more time with. I was tired. I had used up my adrenalin with the spider and the drowning, and now had to go on bare will power. I've always been pretty willful, and now it paid off. As my feet touched the bottom near the far bank, I struggled up a little further and sat down in the river to rest.

In the meantime, a couple of my crew had gotten the work boat and pulled up along side me. I raised my tired arm, pointed to the woods where the bird had disappeared, and let my arm drop back into the water. They pulled the boat into the trees, and one of them jumped out and gave chase. The one driving the boat headed up the river to parallel the bird's course, in case it came back into the water.

I struggled up and followed my partner into the trees. About an hour later we had chased the bird up into and all the way through the main guest area of Silver Springs. The bird started to swim across this small service canal between the main park and the Reptile Institute. As it crossed the canal, a small alligator came off the bank and headed towards it. We stared in fear as the alligator attacked. The gator came up behind the bird, and bit down on the bird's tail.

The bird reached back with its beak, and drove that beak down hard, right between the eyes of that gator. The gator reacted as if it had been blown out of the water. It released the bird and erupted from the water doing a full turn in the air. The gator then dove, and swam off as fast as it could. That was one very surprised gator. The incident allowed us to get close to the bird, and we were finally able to grab it.

We decided to leave the other two cranes in the Giraffe section after that. One day like that is enough for anyone. I know it was for me. After a hot bath and some Bactine for my scrapes and cuts, it was off to sleep, to dream about spiders eating my face.

# Chapter 15: Crocodiles

The Cuban crocodile is one of the meanest members of a group of animals noted for their bad dispositions, the crocodiles. Cuban crocodiles come, not surprisingly, from Cuba. Most of them inhabit one large lake there and, because they do not have a widespread distribution, are considered to be a species with the potential to become extinct very easily. If some catastrophe were to happen to that lake, they would be, in essence, wiped out. Cuban crocodiles have one other endearing characteristic, they are extremely agile. They can jump and can climb quite well. I know this because one night one of them climbed out of its specially designed holding area at Silver Springs and took a walk on the wild side.

Upon arriving at work one morning I was informed by radio that I was needed down by the Cuban croc pen in the Reptile Institute. Upon checking the animals in the institute, the reptile men had noticed one of their crocodiles was missing. It was bad enough to have a few hundred pounds of crocodile of any kind missing, but a Cuban croc was trouble of the worst kind.

Whenever anyone did anything in the pen with the Cuban chocs, like cleaning or landscaping, someone had to stand "shotgun" for him just in case the crocs decided to attack. Our particular escapee was noted for its aggressive nature, and would attack without provocation. You must also realize that in about an hour Silver Springs would open its gates to hundreds of vacationing tourists. These tourists would pour into the park expecting to be entertained, not eaten.

We mounted a massive land and water search for this croc and, fortunately, found it a short distance from its pen in the cypress swamp between the Reptile institute and the Silver River. As I developed the plan for recapturing this animal, those people helping me looked to each other for encouragement. I decided we would ease up on the animal, carefully get two ropes around it's neck, capture it, and carry it back to the pen. Sounds easy, right?...Right! Again, that "capture it" bit was a little vague.

I had one of my people go get me a long piece of PVC pipe. We got the lariats out of the wildlife vehicles, and obtained a burlap bag from the animal compound. We came at the croc from the river side, because the last thing I wanted was for this croc to hit the seven mile long Silver River. Then he would be in his element, and it would be much more difficult to catch him. As we eased up to him, I assigned everyone some specific job.

One of my staff would play a rope out to the left, and one would play a rope out to the right. As we approached the croc, moving very slowly, I could hear my staff choosing which tree they would climb in case the croc charged. The food and beverage manager at the time, a good friend of mine named Mike Jacobs, who had been at the Wildlife Preserve with me, likes to tell the story of how they were all bargaining for trees as we approached the croc. As I said, the plan was to get two ropes on him, secure the animal, and carry it off. This securing bit was really the only hazy part. You see, to secure this animal, I had to jump on its back and hold its mouth shut!

The one good thing about the aggressive nature of the Cuban crocodile is that it isn't afraid of anything. (This is a good thing? You say. In this case, yes.) This factor allowed us to get quite close to the animal without him moving much. He was lying on a small ridge, in the dry area of the cypress swamp. He had his head away from the river, which was good and, as we approached, he lifted his head and tilted it to the right slightly, so that he could keep an eye on us.

I eased up as close as I could to him, and rested one of the lariats lightly on the end of the PVC pipe I had. I eased that pipe out, with the lariat on it, and very slowly maneuvered the noose over the croc's head. He was being very cooperative, just biding his time waiting till someone got close enough for him to attack. The fact that he had raised his head made it much easier for me to get the ropes on him. I laid the rope gently on the back of his neck and drew the PVC pipe back so that I could get the other rope on him. You don't realize how heavy a piece of PVC pipe and a little piece of rope can be until you have to work very slowly with it at arm's length.

The second rope took somewhat longer to place because of the first rope, and because my arms were getting tired from the strain. I finally got the other rope on him, and got ready to give the signal to pull. I had already told my people on the ropes to make absolutely certain that they pull hard, and in unison, and that once they had him, they were to hang on for dear life. I told them to wrap the rope around a tree if they had to, but hang on. I turned and informed the other people present that they might want to stand by their chosen tree, because if one or both of the people on the ropes slipped, or released the rope, we would have one angry croc on one rope, able to move about.

As I gave the countdown for the guys to pull the ropes, the tension mounted. When I said "Three, Two, One, Pull!" The ropes went taut, and the croc reacted with a leap. He tried to roll, which is a natural response in crocodilians, but was prevented from going very far to either side by the straining wildlife people holding the ropes which now secured the croc. I remember the looks on their faces, looks I had seen many times in the animal business, a mixture of strain, accomplishment, and wonder at the reality that here, once again, I had gotten them into some ridiculously dangerous situation. But, for those people it was a simple matter of hanging on, and if anything happened climb a tree. For me, the hard part of my job was about to begin.

As the croc calmed down a bit, I slowly worked my way closer to the croc so that I could cover it's eyes with the burlap sack so that it couldn't see what I was about to do. Remember, the risk to myself was acceptable because there were two ropes on this animal and there were good people on the ropes. But still, something could go wrong, and I could get hurt. (Read the next story to find out just exactly what I am talking about.)

I threw the burlap over his head, and he shook it off. I retrieved the burlap sack with the PVC pipe and tried again. This time my throw was off, and I missed covering his eyes. I tried a third time, and he threw the sack off again. I knew he would eventually get tired of fighting, and tire out, so it was just a matter of time. I threw the burlap sack a forth time. It landed just right, and he just lay there under the sack. I hesitated a moment while I built up some adrenalin, looked around at the people behind me as if to say, "so long," and eased up a little closer. It was so quiet you could hear the rush of the Silver River behind us. When I had worked up enough nerve, I jumped.

I had to position myself just right, because I had to clamp down on those jaws at the same instant I landed on him, or it was bye, bye Frank. I remember aiming for the front of the snout, just behind the nostrils, thinking that I could use the base of those protruding nostrils as a brace against my thumbs. As I came down on him, I wrapped my fingers up under the front of his jaws on either side, and brought my thumbs down behind his nostrils, and grabbed on as hard as I could. I wrapped my legs around his body, just behind his front legs, and held on. I figured I was in for a ride.

The croc reacted with a jump, but thankfully, calmed down immediately. The only problem I had now was that the spot I had chosen to grab happened to be where some of the teeth on this crocodile protruded from the jaw. I had poked a few small holes in my hands as I had grabbed him. This was a minor inconvenience however, and there was no way I was going to let go because of a few scratches. The other people quickly gathered around, being careful not to get too close to the croc's tail. The tail was not secure, and big crocodilians can really do some damage with a blow from their powerful tails. Several of my people jumped on him and held on to the rest of the croc to prevented him from struggling further.

They brought some electrical tape up and we taped the mouth of this big guy shut so that I could finally rest my hands. My hands had cramped so badly due to my desire to hang on as hard as I could, that I had a little trouble opening them for a minute or two. I hadn't really had to hold him that tightly because, as a lot of people know, the crocodilians have a great deal of strength when closing their mouths, but not much strength for opening their mouths. That didn't matter too much to me at the time, however, I was going to hang on with everything I had just in case.

I got up off of the croc and grabbed the head, while several other people grabbed legs, body, and tail, and we lifted him up. As we carried him the short distance back to his pen, we congratulated ourselves for the wonderful job we had done. (We were such a praiseworthy bunch. Tee Hee.) The management was appreciative as well. This was one situation they were glad to see come to such a favorable conclusion.

This wasn't quite the end of the story however, because we still had to take the tape off of him and release him. As we got over to the crocodile pen, I held onto the mouth again while someone cut one side of the tape. It was my intention to grab the end of the tape, and hold on, while we released the croc back into his holding pen, and thus use his weight to help remove the tape.

Unfortunately, the tape was slippery, and my grip wasn't so good, so that when we released him, I only succeeded in pulling the tape off of the top of his mouth. He crawled into his pool and came up with his head on the bank with the remains of that tape still hanging off his lower jaw. It was several hours before it fell off. I did stop by his pen a couple of times to see him that day, and that tape served as a vivid reminder of the exciting events of the morning. My hands still ache a little bit when I think back on how hard I was squeezing that big snout.

The crocodilian display at Silver Springs is impressive. Holding pens had been constructed right in the cypress swamp and, consequently, the animals had very natural habitats which seemed to suit their needs quite nicely. We had eleven different species of crocodilian. Included among these animals was a female gavial, or gahrial, native to India. Gavials are fish-eating crocodiles. They have long,, slender snouts designed for quick, sideways swings. They use this motion to catch fish with their long pointed teeth. The female we had was about ten feet long, and weighed a few hundred pounds.

Gavials are quite rare, and the Indian government has spent a great deal of money and effort in developing captive breeding programs. During a discussion with Howard Hunt, the reptile curator at the Atlanta Zoo, we decided that we would develop the first captive breed-ing program for gavials in this country. It was Mr. Hunt's idea, but I felt that it justified losing one of my display animals for the betterment of the species. The breeding program would take place in a climate con-trolled habitat, especially designed for crocodilians, in the Atlanta Zoo.

This breeding program required that we capture my female gavial, and transport her to the zoo in Atlanta. Mr. Hunt was then going to obtain two male gavials from a zoo in Canada. Moving a gavial involves greater risk to the animal than moving most crocodilians. Since their snout is long and thin, and since their natural defense is to slash their head from side to side, you take the risk that the animal will hit its snout and break it.

Between the two of us, Mr. Hunt was the reptile expert (I had only been in charge of the Reptile Institute at Silver Springs for a few months), consequently, I pretty much let him plan the move. I did design and have built a special crate to carry the gavial. This crate was padded with foam to prevent the gavial from hurting itself, had good handling characteristics, and was made to fit the gavial's exact measurements.

On the day of the move it seemed like every employee in the park was down at the Gavial pen. The plan of attack would be for us to get ropes on her to secure her so that we could go in and grab her and load her in the crate. It was fairly easy to get one rope on her, but as soon as she realized that she was caught she started to fight. She slashed her head from side to side with such force that I just knew she was going to hurt herself.

Mr. Hunt tried to throw a burlap bag over her head, in hopes that if her eyes were covered she would settle down (As the Cuban croc did). Each time that burlap bag came flying, however, she would thrash. She would swing her head violently this way and that and throw that bag off. Finally, I couldn't stand it any longer, and told them to let her calm down. I was very worried that she was going to injure herself. I decided to try to catch her by hand. I took off my boots but left my socks on so that I could get better traction in the mud, and climbed into the pen.

Although she had a rope on her, she was still very mobile, as I was about to find out. She stopped thrashing about, and I eased my way closer to her. She was lying in the shallow area of her pond, near the edge of her pen, out in the open. I slowly worked my way closer to her until I was in position to make an attempt to jump on her, and grab her behind the head. I was not going to grab her by the snout as I had with the Cuban crocodile.

As I slowly moved toward her, she remained very still. Once I had reached my takeoff point, I paused, planning what I would do. I planned to grab this animal behind the neck, and prevent her from turning her head.

Finally, I had worked up enough nerve to make my attempt. As I launched myself towards her, she reacted. She arched her body towards me as I came from her left side. She opened her mouth and caught my left thigh at the same time that I grabbed her behind the head. I knew better than to let go, so, as it happens, I won the war. You see, the first one to let go loses, and she let go first.

After I had her secure, several of the wildlife crew jumped in the pen and grabbed hold of her. We secured her mouth, and as Mr. Hunt got hold of her head, he relegated me to a left rear quarter. I still remember feeling put back on the "back burner" by that move since it was me who caught her I had the crocodile bite to prove it. I have a picture of myself, taken while I was holding onto the gavials hind end. You can see the torn, bloody area on my pants where the gavial bit me.

As I sat there I had several emotions operating at the same time. I was feeling somewhat embarrassed, since I had been bitten, but was quite satisfied that I had caught the animal, and had saved her from potential harm. I was also, as I have said, feeling somewhat "put out" by being supplanted by Mr. Hunt after the excitement was over. Also the people watching from the edge of the pen, my boss Tom Cavanaugh in particular, were concerned for my injury, and I wanted to assure them that I was all right.

Fortunately, the Gavial is a fish eating crocodile with thin jaws. Even though the teeth are formidable, these animals don't have the kind of strength in their jaws you think of when you think of crocodile. Although I still carry the scars of that day, the wounds were not deep, and actually serve as a badge of honor for me. I have other scars. Marks which serve to remind me that I was there, I *did* do those things, that the adventures I have lived are not just some figment of my imagination.

# Chapter 16: Fran, Andy, and Hercules

As I have said, of the four white rhinos we had at the Wildlife Preserve; Bob, Carol, Ted, and Alice; we arranged to keep the larger pair, Bob and Carol, and move them to Silver Springs when the Wildlife Preserve closed. However, we first had to construct a rhino holding area along the Jungle Cruise ride that would contain them. We used a couple of different strategies for constructing the holding area.

The holding pen where the rhinos would spend the night was built like the elephant and rhino pens at the wildlife preserve. It was five strands of elevator cable, laced between telephone poles buried in the ground. We also constructed a shed inside the rhino pen so that the rhinos could get out of the weather.

We wanted the outside area to be more aesthetically pleasing at Silver Springs, so most of the rhino fence was what is called in the animal business, a "ha-ha" fence. A "ha-ha" fence is a fence which is put along the bottom of a ditch. It is called a "ha-ha" fence because the animal thinks there is no fence until it gets up on top of the edge of the ditch. Then, when it sees it is actually fenced in, "ha, ha" on him.

This "ha-ha" fence was also made out of five strands of elevator cable. However, instead of telephone poles as fence posts, we used large galvanized pipe, set in concrete. I remember working down in that ditch, its white sand sides reflecting the hot Florida sun, using a cutting torch to cut holes in the pipes through which the elevator cables would run. It was a hot job. I still have an old pair of glasses I wore when I was cutting those holes. They are full of little pits where the hot metal would splash back in my face because I didn't wear a face shield because it was so hot. Dumb, I know.

The pen was constructed around a small cove along the Jungle Cruise ride and, after we had planted some palms around the outside perimeter and put sod inside, looked pretty good. We were now ready for the Rhinos. We notified Jurgen Shultz that we were ready to receive the rhinos. Jurgen is one of the top animal haulers in the country. I worked with Jurgen, off and on, throughout my entire career, and have a great deal of respect for him. Jurgen and I have been in some situations where we had to trust each other a lot, or something could go very wrong. Jurgen is a big German, who loves life about as much as anyone I have ever met.

The day Jurgen delivered the rhinos was like any other day. Jurgen pulled his big truck down into the service area behind the rhino section as if it were a pickup truck. It is amazing how these guys can maneuver these big trucks in tight places. He got the truck in position for us to remove the two crates containing the rhinos. We were about to go up to get our front end loader to unload the crates, when I noticed that the construction crew that had built the ditch for the "Ha-Ha" fence had left a small bulldozer down near the section.

I said "Wait a minute", and walked over to the bulldozer. Frequently, older heavy equipment will be so worn, or have part of a key broken in the ignition switch, that you can simply insert something in the ignition switch, turn it, and get it to run. Such was the case with this bulldozer. I hopped onto the dozer, started it up, and proceeded to unload the crates.

Jurgen had Carol's crate in the back of the truck, because he wanted the most weight as far forward as possible. That's why he had big Bob's crate in the front of the truck. I pulled Carol's crate out of the truck, and pushed it up to the gate of the rhino holding pen. This gate was one we had brought down from the Wildlife Preserve. It was a large rectangular wooden structure, with wooden supports, crossing like and X, from corner to corner. This gate would play a role in an incident later on but I'll tell you about that in a minute.

We unbolted the metal pipes inside the rhino crate (the ones I described in Amos' chapter) which were located just inside the door facing the holding pen. We opened the doors and Carol came out and began to investigate her new home. We closed the gate while we worked to get Carol's crate moved and Bob's crate off the truck and up to the gate.

Bob was very large at this time and his crate was a full-sized one. The crate had just barely fit in the truck, and was rather difficult to move. Since the crate weighed about a ton, and Bob weighed another three tons, it was quite a job getting the crate out and in position, but we finally did it. We let Bob out of his crate. Bob and Carol had a family reunion and seemed to be quite happy in their new holding pen.

When we let Bob and Carol out into their display area for the first time, they had a ball. They ran around jumping and cavorting. They ran down and walked into the water and, for a minute, I thought they were going to swim off. I didn't know if rhinos could swim, but I could just see me trying to get two rhinos back that had gotten loose in the Florida woods. This vision was soon to come back and haunt me.

The rhinos did so much running and rooting that they soon had our beautiful display area just so much bare sand. Our inability to keep the display looking attractive was the single most important factor in the management's decision to finally get rid of the rhinos. Before we got rid of them, however, we had quite a few interesting moments with them.

Soon after the arrival of the rhinos at Silver Springs, Tom Cavanaugh renamed the Rhinos Andy and Fran, after the head of the Reptile Institute, and his wife. I don't know Tom's motivation, but a name is a name, and we went along with the change. What frequently happens in the animal business is that animals do get their names changed. Usually, if you have a bad animal that you want to get rid of and everyone knows its name and its reputation (Can anyone think of an example? Correct! George.), you change the animal's name, and hope for the best. Not a very nice thing to do, I admit. But it was a common practice.

Not too long after the rhinos arrived at Silver Springs, I went down to check on them first thing in the morning to make sure they were OK. It is always good to make sure your rhinos are where you left them. I drove down to the rhino holding area and got out to check up on them. They were there, looking fairly normal. I noticed, at the back of the shed we had constructed for them, what looked like some kind of splashed water mark on the wall. There had clearly been some fluid sprayed on the wall. There were foamy edges to the spot, and the hay was wet beneath it. I didn't take much notice of it at the time, thinking that maybe one of the rhinos peed on it or something.

When I came back down to the rhino area, about forty-five minutes later, to begin my morning feeding run, where there had been two Rhinos, there were now three. Standing shakily next to Fran was a little baby rhinoceros. He was the cutest, ugliest little thing you have ever seen. I then realized that the fluid that I had seen sprayed on the back of the barn must have been amniotic fluid, where Fran's waters had broken.

If you ever wondered what a rhino would look like without its horn, I can tell you it looks pretty funny, sort of unfinished. You see, the way I figure it, the mother rhinos got together a long time ago and decided that their babies would not have horns when they were born. They figured it was going to be hard enough to give birth to a rhinoceros without having that horn to contend with too.

I made sure everything was OK with our new arrival, and reported the event to my bosses. I then` made a quick trip home to get my 16mm camera, so that I could capture this baby rhino's first day of life on film. He was real cute as he tried to find where the food came from on a mommy that had as much territory to search as Fran did. He kept looking around the front legs, and Fran would gently try to get him back to the back end where the faucets were. Time and time again, he would go for the front legs, and time and time again, Fran would look at him like he was stupid or something. Finally he found the "mother lode."

During the first several days of the baby rhino's life, Andy was compelled to stand quietly down by the gate to the rhino display section. He had to stand quietly down there, because if he made any kind of move, Fran would be on him like a duck on a June bug. She wanted to make absolutely certain that daddy didn't hurt her baby. She was a very good mother.

Silver Springs had a contest to name the baby rhino. I remember it was down to three choices when they came to me to ask me my opinion. We picked Hercules over the other two which, if memory serves me correctly were something like "Horny" and "Frandy." Hercules he was. Hercules grew steadily, and my long time relationship with these rhinos allowed me to interact with these rhinos much more closely than most other people had been able to interact with other rhinos.

I had gotten to know Andy quite well over the past three years. (Remember, I had spent time with him in the elephant section of the Wildlife Preserve.) He was a very docile animal anyway. However, with a little patience, I got to the point where I could get right up next to him without him getting upset. I started to pet him and scratch him on the soft skin around his neck and front leg. At some point I found out that he, like most other animals, loved having his belly scratched.

Now, let me paint a picture for you again. Here was 6000 pounds of African White Rhino, standing over five feet tall. And here was 200 pounds of human, standing just about the same height. I would start to scratch Andy's armored hide with my hand. He would extend his head for me to rub under his neck, and extend his back leg, for me to get to his stomach. If I continued to scratch his belly, he would try to get more of his belly exposed, and would eventually fall right over. That's right, fall over. The first time he did this, I was worried that he had an attack of some kind, but no, he just wanted his belly scratched.

He would lie there on his back like some gigantic dog until I stopped scratching him. Then he would struggle to get back on his feet and go on about his business of being a rhino. It was one of the most unbelievable things I ever gotten an animal to do, and was one of my favorite "show off" routines. My bosses would bring VIPs down and have me make Andy fall over for them. My ability to amuse this animal was not shared by everyone however.

One day, when I was otherwise occupied, my boss went down to the rhino section with someone to impress. He got into the pen with the rhinos, and proceeded to try to scratch Andy's belly. Andy apparently would have nothing of it and, hooking my boss up under his thigh, threw him out of the pen. My boss was none the worse for wear, except maybe for his pride, but he let me do the "showing off" with the rhinos from then on.

With all the attention I gave Andy, and with a great deal of tolerance by Fran, Hercules soon became a big pet. He was about eighty pounds at birth, and as I said, grew rapidly. Hercules was a typical kid. He loved to run, and jump, and play.

Play to a animal is designed to prepare them for a life of interaction with their own kind. Rhinos fight with each other using their horns. Consequently, Hercules would want to butt you with the front of his face (he didn't have a horn when he was young remember). The only trouble with this was that eighty-plus pounds moving fast at about thigh height was difficult to defend against.

Hercules didn't know how strong he was, and probably didn't care. It took me a long time to get him to ease up on his play so that he didn't flatten me right away. Fortunately, he got the message before he started to grow his horn, or I would have really been in trouble.

It turned out Hercules was just like his dad in one respect, he loved having his belly scratched. And, just like his dad, would actually fall right over when you did it. I can't impress upon you strongly enough how strange it was to see these huge animals just keel over. It was if they had been knocked out by some invisible giant. Well, Hercules grew and grew, and when we finally got rid of the rhinos at Silver Springs, he weighed about 2000 pounds.

There were many days of wonder with the rhinos before they left Silver Springs. One day I remember vividly. One Saturday I was getting a well deserved day off (Pretty smug Huh….Sorry!), when the phone awoke me from a deep sleep. I have mentioned that the ringing of the phone set my adrenalin flowing immediately, because I never knew what dangers would follow. The voice on the line said, "We need you to come in to work, the rhinos are loose."

I hopped out of bed, got dressed, and hurried to work. When I got there it wasn't difficult to find someone, people were driving all over the place. I drove down to the rhino section, and saw that the wooden gate which led out from the holding pen was in a shambles. It was broken up so badly that we took it off its hinges in pieces. It seems that the wood had rotted somewhat, and the rhinos had simply destroyed it.

We knew the rhinos were somewhere in about 2000 acres of Florida scrub land adjacent to Silver Springs. This area did have a fence around it, a four foot high, chain-link fence. After having seen what the rhinos did to the massive rhino gate, I knew that little chain-link fence would be light work for them if the rhinos wanted to go through it.

We had vehicles all over the area, and were in constant contact by radio. They had seen Fran and Hercules prior to my getting there, but kept losing them as they would go cross country into areas where the vehicles couldn't go. We found Andy soon after. It was our intent to work the rhinos down toward the holding pen and coax them in. We soon found out this was much easier said than done.

We worked for hours in the hot Florida sun and finally got the three rhinos back together. We had not necessarily tried to do it, but our paths crossed as one group of us moved Andy and the other group moved Fran and Hercules. We tried and tried to work them back towards the holding pen, but we just couldn't get them to go where we wanted them to go. Most of the time the rhinos were in the bushes or trees, and couldn't be driven by vehicle, so had to be driven on foot. Believe me, as well as I knew these rhinos, if they turned and decided they wanted to go back the way they had come, I would let them. I wasn't going to stand in front of a determined rhino and tell it "No!"

After getting the rhinos close to the holding pen many times, we were getting desperate. At about four o'clock in the afternoon the rhinos just seemed to decide to go through an area they had refused to go through about fifty times before, and we had them. The relief which went through the group was exceeded only by our fatigue as we pulled a vehicle up to block off the now wide open gate opening.

We built a makeshift wall to block off the gate opening until I could go up to the maintenance area and build a new gate. I built this new gate out of galvanized pipe welded together. It was strong and heavy, and served us well for the remainder of the time the rhinos were at Silver Springs.

It is sometimes frightening to realize the possibilities one faces in the animal business. The thought of animal escape haunted us daily. In our attempt to make the animals as happy and comfortable as possible, we also had to be acutely aware of our responsibility to our community. It was our duty to keep the animals where they are supposed to be, healthy, and happy. For the most part, we did our jobs admirably. Those times we did not served to remind us of the awesome responsibility we shouldered.

# Chapter 17: Silver Springs Hoofstock

I would like to close this book with a chapter about hoofstock. This chapter has birth and death, success and failure, humor and tragedy. It sums up my eleven years in the animal business. It describes the business and the man as they were, no frills, just one person trying to do the best he could do.

One day in spring at Silver Springs, I took my fairly young crew down to the main animal holding area. This was a day that I had set aside for two specific reasons. The first reason was that the weather in Florida was beginning to warm up and, consequently, it was time to shear the llamas. A llama has a beautiful, thick coat of fine hair which, when made into rugs or clothes, is as soft as eider down.

However, this thick coat of hair does not do them any good during the hot Florida summers. So, every spring, we sheared the llamas. The other reason for this day's exercise was for me to teach my staff how to rope. Yes, throw a lariat rope just like a cowboy. Well, that was the intent.

We got down to the holding area and got set up. I had a generator sitting in the back of my Bronco to power the clippers we would use to trim the wool off the llamas. I decided to begin to show my crew how to rope llamas using one of the llamas that was easy to handle. We could have simply caught this animal, but there was a lesson to be learned here, so roping was the course of action. Little did I know at the time, that the lesson intended was not the lesson that would be taught.

I stationed my people parallel to one of the fence lines and ran the chosen llama down into the corner. My people formed a line, which, with the opposing fence line that they were facing, formed a corridor down which I would run the llama for the roping attempt. The llama I had chosen was the largest one we had. He was a big male and, as I have said, good natured. So, while I explained what I was going to do, he waited patiently in the corner.

I told my people, who were all very attentive, thinking that they would soon be the recipients of some great hidden knowledge, to watch very carefully. I told them that the idea was to hold unto the knot end of the rope, and loosely coil the majority of the rope up in that hand, (For me that would be my left hand because I am right handed). With the other hand (my right), grab the loop of the lariat and a bit of the trailing rope, just below the "hondo." The "hondo" is a breakaway device which lets you release the rope without having to pull it back over the animal's head.

I showed them how to slowly rotate the open loop above your head, keeping the noose as opened as possible. I instructed them that, as the animal passed, you were to release the lariat trying to let that open noose fall just in front of the animal, so that the animal's head go through the opening and the noose slides down on the animals neck. I said, "I know that is difficult to picture, so just watch for a few times. Watch the loop of the rope."

Finally, I was ready. They were ready. The llama was ready. So, I began. We finally got the llama moving, and he turned on the speed as he ran past me. I was rotating the loop above my head being the very picture of a cowboy. As he ran past me, I threw the perfect throw, and the loop went out and down over the llamas neck. I guess I was so glad that I had not made a fool out of myself by missing the llama, that I was lost in thought for a moment. I had neglected to remember that the roping part was only the first step. I still had a llama to catch.

With my left hand tightly gripping my end of the rope, the llama quickly pulled his loop end tight. Well, just like you see in the cartoons, off I went across the field. Oh, I wasn't running after this llama. You see, he had pulled me slap off my feet. Consequently, I was being dragged along behind this llama, flat on my belly, skidding and bumping my way across the field.

I can vividly recall looking over to my left and seeing my crew. I was seeing them sideways, but I knew what they were doing. They were all, to a person, either bent over double or rolling on the ground laughing. I will never forget the thoughts rushing through my mind during those fleeting moments.

As I saw more and more of them fall in laughter, I can remember thinking that this really must be a pretty funny sight. This big male llama trailing a rope, on the end of which hung this short, stocky, formerly very professional, animal man. I remember smiling as I wondered if anyone would recover quickly enough to give me some help. That problem became moot in a moment, because the llama quickly got tired of dragging my dead weight and stopped. As I got back to my feet, bracing them so I could avoid another free ride, some of my staff recovered enough to help me secure the llama.

They were still laughing. I brushed what I could of the grass and dirt from the entire length of my body. Someone said, "If that's how you rope an animal, we'd rather not learn how." I said, "Very funny." and off we went to try to finish our job of shearing llamas. This was another of those times that I wish there had been movie cameras operating. I would love to have seen the scene that gave my crew such pleasure.

If ostriches are my least favorite animal, running a close second are camels. Camels aren't quite as stupid as ostriches, not quite, but they make up for this disadvantage by having about ten times the stubbornness. Camels can get quite large as well. They have two pairs of incisors in their upper jaw, and canines top and bottom, and can give you a very nasty bite. I know this from personal experience.

I have been told that camels like to spit. I have never personally seen a camel spit, but I'm sure they do. They seem to enjoy working up a good mouthful of slime at the least provocation, however. From working with llamas, who do spit for sure, I know that when these camelids go down into their stomach to bring up a good wad of spitting material the delivered product is quite unpleasant.

One camel I had particular trouble with was called Clyde, what else? Since Ray Stevens came out with the song "Ahab, The Arab", most camels have been named Clyde. Clyde was a fairly young camel, only a few years old, but had grown quickly, and stood about six and a half to seven feet tall. He had a disposition somewhat like that of an ostrich. He was OK one minute, and nuts the next. We learned to stay away from him, for the most part, because he was big and potentially dangerous.

One day, when we were fixing the fence down near his section, one of my employees forgot to watch Clyde closely enough. We were working on the fence, and not paying much attention to Clyde who was in the pen next to us. It seemed that Clyde was very jealous and spoiled, and when you didn't pay any attention to him, he got himself worked up. He also got worked up when anyone was catching animals anywhere around him, but I'll tell you about that in a minute.

This young employee of mine was sitting on the ground, hammering staples into a fence post in order to attach the fence to the post, I looked over and saw Clyde bent down, grab him by the thigh, and lifted him high in the air. This fellow was a little better than six feet tall, and weighed about 180 pounds, and Clyde lifted him like he was nothing. Well, he yelled and I got up to rush over and help him. Just about that time, Clyde dropped him, and he landed with a thud back on the ground. He scrambled up and away from Clyde. I asked him if he was hurt. He said "No." And back we went to work, somewhat more watchful of the excited Clyde.

As I said, Clyde was sort of off again, on again, and so there were times when you could be around him. One day I was in the African hoof stock section along the Jungle Cruise ride at Silver Springs, when my boss came down with some public relations people. They wanted to get some photographs. Photographs were more important in selling Silver Springs to the public than were a bunch of goofy wildlife handlers. This was a truth none of us ever really liked to acknowledge.

As a matter of fact, most of the really bad times I ever had in the animal business were due to conflicts with the public relations departments. We usually disagreed about what they wanted the animals to do, as compared to what I was willing to have the animals do. I would rather fight with George than to try to argue with a public relations person.

Anyway, these people wanted some shots of the giraffes, and I was to get the giraffes into perfect picture position. Clyde was in the section at that time, and I was out there on foot. As I was talking to my boss and the people he had with him, I didn't notice Clyde move up right behind me.

My boss and the PR people were on the other side of the fence, so were not in any danger. As I was trying to figure out what the photographers wanted, I saw a big grin come over my boss's face. A look of fear mixed with amazement came unto the faces of the PR people. I knew what that meant from several years in the animal business, so, as I turned, I instinctively threw my left arm up to protect myself, and there was Clyde. He bit down on my upper left arm, and picked me up.

As I watched my boss curl up in laughter, and the mouths of the PR people gape open, I punched Clyde on the nose with my right hand, and rolled out of his mouth. Fortunately, neither his incisors nor his canines had penetrated my flesh too deeply, so I only got a couple of scratches where I had rolled off of his bottom teeth. I jumped over the gate and went over to my boss, who was still in stitches, and said "Thanks a lot for the warning!" He just grinned wider and said, "You're welcome." We are such a fun bunch in the animal business.

That wasn't the most memorable time I had with Clyde, however. As I tell *this* story, remember that camels have this extremely sticky saliva that they work into a foam. It gets all around their mouths, as if they were some kind of giant mad dog. And if that isn't bad enough, they can inflate their soft palate, which then protrudes from their mouth, and gurgle this stuff all over themselves. They also have a habit of shaking their heads when they have this stuff all over them, and it flies around like some kind of saliva from hell with a mind of its own. With those thoughts in mind, on with the story.

I was catching llamas, one fine spring day, in order to move them into an area where we could do some health testing. Most of them moved very easily as we drove them up through their gate and into the holding area. But, as usual, there are always a couple of hard heads in the bunch, and I had to rope them. Roping llamas isn't very difficult, if you are a good roper, and I wasn't.(But then you already know that, now don't you?) My roping was a little like Clyde's personality, off and on. I was, however, good enough for it to pay us to try to catch a couple of llamas that way. So we did.

All the time we had been catching llamas, Clyde had been in the pen next to us. He had been working himself up more and more. He had slime all over him. We could see this slime dotted all along the ground, the fence, and half a dozen trees along the fence row where he was raging back and forth.

To catch the llamas, we would run the llamas down that same fence line where they would be forced to go past me, and I would try to rope them. When we finally got to the last llama, I threw a pretty good toss and I roped it. However, since the llama outweighed me a couple times over, it pulled me along with it. This is normal. The roping is just to get the animal slowed down enough so that we could all run over and grab it and walk it wherever it was supposed to go.

This was the last llama, and I had roped it with only one throw, so I was pretty self-occupied with how well I had done. (Looking back on it, it seems like I would have been a better roper if I had not been as successful as I was, on those rare occasions when I was successful.) Being thus lost in thought, I did not realize that the llama had pulled me over next to the fence behind which raged Clyde.

I can remember the sensation of this large mass moving down over me, and the next thing I knew, I was up to my ears in camel. Or, should I say down to my ears? Clyde had bitten down on my head, so that my head was in his mouth, and his front teeth were down to where my ears were. I remember yelling, dropping to the ground, and rolling out of the way.

I looked over to see Clyde eating my Silver Springs baseball cap, and realized that cap had probably saved my precious head. As Clyde bit down on my head, his saliva lubricated my cap and it slipped off when I dropped. This momentary introspection was postponed when I realized my head was coated in camel slime. I handed the rope to one of my people, (Yes, like a true animal man I hadn't let go of the llama.) and headed for the canal. The Jungle Cruise ride at Silver Springs goes down a canal, on the banks of which we developed the animal display areas.

I jumped into the canal, boots and all, and proceeded to use the sand from the river bank to scrub that thick coating of camel slime from my head and hair. It was no easy task, but when I finally succeeded in removing enough of it for comfort, I looked up and saw my crew still laughing at the scene they had just witnessed. Like I said, we're a fun bunch in the animal business. I am so glad I served as a ready source of amusement for a group of people who worked as hard as my crew did.

Giraffes are my favorite of all the hoof stock. They seem to be fairly intelligent, and can become quite tame. They are also quite impressive when you are in a group of them and you are only five foot six. I could walk right under the bellies of several of them I had.

We had a breeding herd of Giraffes at Silver Springs. I have worked around many giraffes, but the ones I had at Silver Springs I hold most dear. One of the best of the bunch was Bonnie. She was the first giraffe to have a baby at Silver Springs.

Bonnie was a female giraffe who had a long scar on her neck where she had cut herself when she was young. As I said, Bonnie was our first mother giraffe. We started to notice that Bonnie was putting on weight, and hoped that she was pregnant. Bonnie grew and grew and, after many months, one day we noticed that her mammary glands were filling up.

We put her in the holding area up at the giraffe barn, and waited. We were anticipating the happy event any moment. Bonnie kept us waiting for about a week. One morning I went down to the barn to check on Bonnie, and noticed that she wasn't acting like she usually did. She wasn't excited to see me, and was simply standing very still, with her ears folded back against her head.

I figured it was about time for the baby to come, so I hurried back up to the wildlife office to place a call to the veterinarian and inform my boss, Tom Cavanaugh. I then went back down to wait for the birth. I had never seen a giraffe being born before, and was really looking forward to it. Bonnie kept us waiting for about four hours. Then she started to push.

The first thing out were these two dark gray looking lumps that we soon identified as front feet. As Bonnie would push, in time with her contractions, we would see more and more of the baby exposed, inch by inch. The hooves were followed, not surprisingly, by several inches of front legs. Finally, we could see the nose of the baby start to emerge.

With an extra special push, Bonnie got the head of this baby out, and everything stopped right there. Oh, Bonnie would continue to push, but nothing was moving. We found out later, when we had problems with a giraffe named Wadsworth (you'll read about her in a little bit), that the chest is the most trouble for a giraffe to pass, everything else is long and skinny.

I was really getting worried because the baby's head was beginning to turn blue, and its tongue was hanging out of its mouth. Just about the time that I had decided I was going to go in and help deliver that baby, Bonnie gave a mighty push, and out popped five and a half feet of legs and neck. Bonnie had not lain down to have this baby. That's right, giraffes have their babies standing up, and the first thing a baby giraffe does is fall about five feet.

That baby landed in a great big pile of legs and neck which seemed not to have any solid bones at all. Bonnie immediately turned and licked the baby's face, and the baby responded by raising its head. Bonnie didn't clean the baby up very well, and we came to realize this was a characteristic of this particular giraffe. I don't blame her much though, I don't think I would want to eat afterbirth either, especially coated with slime and dirt.

In about an hour, the baby finally got to its feet, and immediately started looking for the nozzles where the food came from. It found them, after searching all over Bonnie for about a half an hour. The scene which followed is indelibly etched in my memory. Mother and daughter, (Yes, she was a little female.) both with looks of great satisfaction on their faces. Bonnie turned out to be a very good mother, and had several more babies at Silver Springs.

One of the other giraffes we had at Silver Springs was not such a good mother. Oh, she was good at having babies, but she didn't want anything to do with them after she had them. Her name was Alice. Alice was a moody giraffe who never really did get what I would call friendly. She wasn't aggressive, just not friendly.

When we decided that Alice was finally pregnant, we kept a watch on her. After while, her milk finally dropped, and we put her up in the holding area of the giraffe barn. Everything went about like it had gone with bonnie, except Alice stopped pushing when only the baby's front feet were exposed. We waited for quite some time before I decided to pull the baby manually.

We got Alice into the Giraffe barn, and my assistant Scott Sutton and I got in with her. She was understandably upset, but was not acting too aggressively. As she turned, Scott and I tried to grab the baby's feet which were sticking out of the back end of Alice. The feet slipped out of our hands on the first try. They were so slippery we had to grab a hand full of hay for traction, and try again. As we got a good grip on the baby's feet, Alice realized something was up. (That's not surprising, all things considered.)

As we pulled on those feet, Alice would rock forward and try to push the baby out. After one or two of these tugs-of-war, the baby came out in a rush. We immediately left Alice alone with her baby, and watched from the sidelines. Alice cleaned her babies up much better than Bonnie did, but her motherhood stopped there. As the baby took its first steps to try to find the desperately needed milk, Alice got nasty. She started to push the baby away, and finally started trying to kick it.

I got Alice out of there in a hurry, and decided we were stuck with raising a baby giraffe. This thought elicited mixed emotions in me. I really wanted to raise a giraffe, but I was concerned with my ability to do so successfully. Anyway, we were stuck with her now.

This little giraffe turned out to be a whole lot of trouble. Oh she was a little doll, but she went through some tough times. When she was just a few weeks old, she got a urinary infection. This infection caused her to strain when she peed, and she prolapsed her rectum during one of the times she was straining.

I got the Vet in right away and we reinserted the prolapse It had been the mucosa of her descending colon. The Vet then took a couple of light sutures to keep it in place. We put her on antibiotics, which we were finally able to give to her in her milk. She was the pickiest eater of any animal I have ever bottle raised (Except maybe for Go-Goat). She could tell if there was even a trace of something else in her milk.

After a few days, the damaged mucosa started to slough off, and she got badly infected. I was forced to give her injectable antibiotics. She worsened to the point where she would not get up. One afternoon she was lying in the barn, and she just rolled over on her side and lay there.

I ran over and struggled to get her up. She weighed about two hundred pounds. She would respond for a while, and hold herself up. Then she would collapse back down again. Just about the time I thought I was going to loose her for sure, she started to perk up.

I pushed her up one last time, and she struggled to her feet. As she stood there wobbling, I offered her her bottle, which she hadn't taken for three days. She smelled it, then latched onto the nipple and drank it down. I was greatly relieved.

She simply grew stronger and stronger after than. Eating, and drinking her bottle. I sort of spoiled her by continuing to give her a bottle well into her second year. I have pictures of myself standing up on the bed railing of my Bronco, my arm as high as it can reach, with S.G. bending slightly to get her bottle. S.G. was what I named her. It stands for Super Giraffe.

Wadsworth was a giraffe who seemed to follow me wherever I went. When I was at Lion Country, she was one of the giraffes I would see when I was walking my elephants around the hoofstock section. I didn't really know her as a personality then, but I came to know her quite well later on. After I moved to The Wildlife Preserve, we purchased Wadsworth, and she became part of our giraffe herd there. When I moved to Silver Springs, Wadsworth was one of the giraffes we acquired for our African exhibit on the Jungle Cruise ride. All together I was with Wadsy (her nickname), for ten of my eleven years in the animal business.

Wadsworth was, by the time she got to Silver Springs, a large female, fourteen feet tall, with a mind of her own. She was very pushy, literally. She would push on just about anything if she thought it was in her way. She would push on gates, fences, vehicles, and even you if you gave her the chance. Except for that hard-headedness, she was a likable animal and didn't cause *too* much trouble.

One day, I noticed Wadsworth standing very still on the ridge above the Jungle Cruise ride. She had her back feet set fairly wide apart, and I went over to investigate. I saw a bit of tissue hanging from her vulva. We had not thought that she was pregnant, but since she was so big anyway, I thought there might be a possibility. I isolated her in the giraffe barn, and called the vet. He came out and looked at her. He thought that she might be pregnant also, and that we ought to give her till the next day before we got concerned.

The next morning Wadsworth's condition was unchanged. I called the vet again, and we decided to tranquilize her to see what the problem was. As I have mentioned before, tranquilizing giraffes requires some special considerations. Not only did we have to make certain that we kept her head above her stomach, but we had to worry about how she was going to go down inside a barn. We got her inside the giraffe barn, which was a large four-by-four and plywood structure, with a wooden fence separating the inside into two sections. This separation was about six feet high.

We darted her with the tranquilizer, and stood back to let it take effect. Unfortunately, it took effect as she was turning around during her pacing. She got her feet caught up in each other and fell sideways. Fortunately, she fell against the separating fence, and as it gave way, it sort of took the brunt of her fall. I immediately got someone to hold up her head, and the Vet and I got to work. She was not completely knocked out though, so the other members of my crew had to alternate holding her head. Since she was moving her head and neck around so much, holding her head up really tired you out.

The vet got to feeling up inside her, and confirmed that she was indeed pregnant. Unfortunately, the baby had had its head bent back too much in the final stages of pregnancy, and the baby was dead. It had also been several days since this had happened, and the baby had started to decompose. Everyone was hit by the smell of that decomposing baby when the vet removed his hand from Wadsworth's body. Several of my staff had to run around to the outside of the barn for a breath of fresh air. This new factor made holding the head an even more unpleasant task.

The vet and I worked to try to get the baby in a position so that we could get a delivery chain on it, and pull it out with a device known as a calf puller. This is a chain operated device that, when placed against the rear end of a cow and hooked to the delivery chain, can be used to pull a baby out of the cow. The vet finally got the chain around the front feet and head of the baby, and began to crank the calf puller. The calf puller has a broad curved base that goes against the rear end of the cow, and you turn the handle to pull the chain as you hold the machine up and guide the calf out.

The vet was cranking the calf puller when, like a shot, the chain broke. We were at a loss as to what to do when I remembered I had a two ton comealong in the jeep. A comealong is a system of gears and pulleys, yo which a cable is attached. Using the handle, and using a ratchet system to prevent the cable from backing up, the comealong is designed to cause things to "come along." We used it to pull fencing so that it could be tightened and stapled to the fence posts. You can also use it to pull vehicles out of the mud or sand, if you attach it to a tree or another vehicle.

We ran the comealong out of the barn and attached it to the fence. As we carefully took the comealong up, one notch at a time, the vet worked, and worked, to get the dead baby out of Wadsworth. Wadsworth, in the meantime, would strain every time we pulled, and I know it was agony for her. Giraffes don't make any vocalizations beyond a sort of a rumble, and at that moment I was glad they didn't. I just know she would have been screaming if she could have.

We finally got the baby's head and neck out, but the chest was so big that it got hung up. With the decaying head out in the open, most of my staff had headed for the clear breeze on the other side of the giraffe barn. To tell you the truth, the Vet had to get a breath of fresh air every now and then. Also, I guess I was blessed with a pretty strong stomach, so I would hold the head while everyone else was recovering.

We decided to make one big final effort because Wadsworth's life was at stake. She had been tranquilized for a long time, it was getting hot, and the stress she had been under was monumental. We gave the comealong a couple of more clicks. The vet did an episiotomy (cutting the vaginal opening), and out the baby came.

We packed Wadsworth with antibiotic suppositories, sewed her up, and gave her the drug which would bring her back to full consciousness. Wadsworth had been down for so long, and was stretched out so completely, that she couldn't get her right legs up under her body and, consequently, couldn't stand up. She tried and tried, but she just couldn't do it. I had my people run in and push on the right side of her body when she strained to get up, but she still couldn't get up.

I realized that we would have to get her right rear leg up under her body before she would be able to get herself balanced enough to get up. I went around to the belly side of her. I lay down on my back, with my hands stretched out over my head pressed against the squeeze chute behind me. I slowly eased my feet up under her belly to her right rear leg. I hooked her leg with my boot heels, right above her right foot.

With Giraffe legs flying above my prone form from time to time, I pushed with my legs, thus forcing her right rear leg up under her body. As she made one more effort to right herself, my crew pushed as hard as they could on her right side while I pushed as hard as I could on her right leg. She made a huge effort to get her foot under her and succeeded. In a moment she was up, somewhat unsteadily, but up.

Unfortunately, the ordeal wasn't over yet. Our fears of infection were justified. Wadsworth had not eaten since I had put her in the barn, and I was worried about her condition. A couple of days after pulling the dead baby from her, I noticed some clotty white discharge. I knew she was infected. I called the vet, and told him what I had seen. He prescribed injectable antibiotics, also injectable vitamins and iron since she was not eating well. I was to give her the two shots, every eight hours, round the clock.

I had had a giraffe squeeze cage installed in the barn some time ago, and I began the series of shots with Wadsworth in the confined space of the cage. This worked fairly well, when the needle didn't bend or the syringe didn't break because of the tough hide of this giraffe. But after a while, Wadsworth didn't like to go into the chute for her shot. At those times, I would simply put her in the barn. I would hang from the hay feeder with my left hand, and try to get the shot in her butt as she paced by. This became a great game with her, and she took delight in avoiding the shots.

Every now and then, however, she would get an attitude like, "Well, let's get this over," and actually back up to me, and stand for her shot. As I have said, these shots were every eight hours round the clock. I had a fellow working for me whose name was Blake Rutland, and he would give the shots for me when I got too tired to make the appointment. Blake lost his life in an automobile accident shortly after that, and I can't help but recall him when I think of Wadsworth. Blake was a dear friend, and a great animal handler, and I will never forget him.

During the weeks of treatment, Wadsworth rarely ate. About the only thing she would seem to take were the cookies I used to bring her from the food service area. If I stood there and fed her cookies, or bread, she would eat, however, she didn't eat much of anything by herself. Blake would also take her down bread or cookies from time to time. I think these few things were the only things that sustained her.

After three long months of shots and hand feeding, I was at the pen one day when Wadsworth seemed to say "Well, if you guys aren't going to give up on me, I might as well not give up on myself." She started eating regularly that day, and improved daily. She gained back all the weight she had lost, several hundred pounds, and looked like our old Wadsworth again.

She never did get pregnant again while I was at Silver Springs, but the vet and I figured that there had been too much damage done, and we were just glad that she had survived. However, a couple of years after I had left Silver Springs, I was talking to my old assistant, Steve Shurter, and he told me that Wadsworth had conceived again and had given birth to a healthy little baby giraffe. The news was a catharsis. Blake was gone, but Wadsworth had survived to become a healthy happy mother. It was part of Blake's life force which had helped her to survive, and it still lived on in her.

Let me leave you with a couple of vignettes about sheep, nothing fancy, just sheep. Mouflons are the big-horned sheep originally found wild on the islands in the Mediterranean. The males are dark brown, shading to a black stripe on their flanks, and black on their upper legs. They have whitish bellies and lower legs. Adult males have a large mane of hair which extends out and down from their chest. Females are a uniform brown all over. All of the members of the sheep family interbreed quite readily, so there has been a significant amount of crossbreeding among the wild sheep in captivity. Consequently, the original sizes and appearances of these sheep have been altered on occasion.

I worked with mouflon throughout my career. They were fairly cheep, easy to work with, and made a good display. These factors made them very popular with the management. The big males would get the large curved horns everybody is used to seeing on the Rocky Mountain big-horned sheep.

It has always amazed me to watch those big sheep butt heads like they do. You would think that they would knock themselves senseless. They don't, of course, because they are physiologically designed to take that kind of punishment, and keep on going. They have a sort of a shock absorber system in their necks to prevent them from taking too much damage. On a couple of occasions, however, their horns got some of their owners in trouble.

In 1978, I quit smoking, and shortly after that, weighed over 200 pounds. I am stocky to begin with, but that much weight was a burden. The only thing I liked about being that heavy was that I was pretty strong, too. I made the decision to lose some weight, and, about four months later, I was down below 160 pounds. I won't go into how I did it, here, I'll save that for my diet book. (Why not, everyone else is writing one).

After I lost the weight, I felt very healthy, but I also felt a lot weaker than I had been. One warm sunny afternoon, when I was going down to the giraffe barn for something, I noticed this big male mouflon standing in the trees down inside the holding pen where the giraffe barn was located. I went through the gate and could see that this mouflon had gotten itself wound around a small tree somehow. It had gotten that tree up inside the coil of its right horn, and couldn't get itself unwound.

The mouflon in question was a big male, well over one hundred pounds. When I had been heavy, it would have been nothing for me to just go over, unscrew that mouflon, and walk him anywhere I wanted him to go. It was with that frame of mind that I approached him to get him loose.

I had decided that, since he was caught, and I was going to sell some surplus mouflon soon anyway (They breed real well in captivity and soon overpopulate their section.), I would simply get this mouflon loose, walk him over to a holding pen, put him in and hold him for sale.

I walked over to him, and he was understandably nervous. He was bouncing, and trying to get himself untangled from that tree, but was having no luck. He was really stuck. I finally got up to him, and grabbed him to keep him from breaking his neck or something else.

I then proceeded to try to get him unscrewed from that tree. I had to push the tree and twist him, as I tried to move the tree around, so that I could get him unscrewed. All the time I am trying to get him loose, he is trying to get loose from me. So I'm pulling one way, and he's pulling the opposite way, and I'm getting nowhere fast.

Finally he got still for a moment. I was able to push the tree real hard, and, finally, he came loose. I grabbed hold of his horns for what I thought was, now, a simple task of walking him down to the holding pen. No such luck! He realized he was free, and off we went. He started running, and it was all I could do to hang on. I figured that I had made a decision to move this animal and, by golly, I would move him. It turns out that he had also made a decision, to move me. He seemed to be having much more success at following through on his decision than I was having following through on mine.

He ran me around the field for a several minutes, jumping and running, now charging, now backing up. He finally ran me out into the middle of the hard packed dirt road, and charged toward me again. I was so tired by that time that he knocked me off my feet, and we went down in a big pile, me lying on my back holding on to him. In a flash, he jumped up, and kind of drove into me pushing me down the road several feet. At this point, my arms were all skinned up, I was tired and sore, and was just about ready to give up.

I gave one last twist of his horns and pulled him over part way on top of me. We just lay there, both of us struggling to catch our breath. I could feel the heat from his body as he lay there breathing heavily. I got a nose full of his strong, sweet, gamy, smell, mixed with the smell of our sweat. I started to talk to him as we lay there in the middle of the road, sweating and dirty. I told him that I had no intention of giving up and that I was bound and determined to get him into that holding pen. I said he would be taken to a real nice place and he would have lots of pretty young female mouflon to play with.

I guess my talk worked, or he was as worn out as I was. As I struggled to my feet and got him to his, he seemed to concede defeat. I started out towards the holding pen, ready for the next round, if necessary, but it wasn't necessary. After only a couple of half-hearted tries at escape, he gave up, and the trip to the holding pen was concluded without a hitch. I slid the door open with my left hand as I held the mouflon with my right. I grabbed the mouflon shoved him in the pen, slid the door closed, and sat down on the ground. It was some little time before I could get up and get us both some water.

There is one last story I want to tell. One morning, I was making my morning run on the canal to feed the island with the zebras, sarus cranes, and the one ostrich, and open the gate for the Jungle Cruise boats. As I have said, those morning trips down the Silver River were some of the best times I have ever had. The mist would rise from that warm water, giving the river a mystical appearance. The animals would be waking and giving voice to their morning songs. The gurgle of the water against the hull of my boat beat a lullaby to me as I traveled.

As I passed the mouflon section, I noticed two of the large males fighting. I slowed the boat down, and watched them for a minute because they were not acting normally. Normally they back up and butt heads like you have seen those Rocky Mountain big-horns do. These guys were running around in circles with their heads together. I pulled the boat up alongside the canal, turned the motor off, and got out.

I finally saw what the problem was. These two big males had gotten their horns wound around each other's horns, and couldn't get loose. I contemplated going for help, but the way these animals were pulling and pushing, I really thought one or both of them might break a neck soon. The way they were tangled forced one, or both of them, to get his neck bent back sharply when either one of them would take off in one direction or the other. I made the decision to try to get them free myself. Little did I know what I was getting into.

As I approached them, they noticed me and got even more frantic. Fortunately for me they were working at cross purposes, and couldn't get into sync enough to take off in any one direction for long. As they circled each other, jumping and pushing, I was able to close the distance between us, and get up to them. As they made another circle, I grabbed them. I grabbed for the usual handles you use when moving male mouflon, the horns. Unfortunately, these horns had other horns attached to them, and I soon found out that maybe it wasn't such a good idea to stick my hands in that mess after all.

They started jumping and running in circles. Now, instead of two animals hooked together, there were three. The only problem was that the third animal was not ready for the ride. They were bashing and grinding their horns together, and my hands were in the middle of it. It was just a couple on seconds before my fingers were all skinned up.

I tried to get these two excited animals apart for several minutes. I tried pushing one of their heads down, while I lifted the other one. I tried pushing one forward, while I pulled the other one back. Nothing seemed to make any difference. They where screwed together a full 360 degrees. I didn't know how I was going to rotate one of them sideways in a full circle, while holding the other one still.

The mouflon on the far side of me made the decision to push, and this worked to my advantage. I got my knees up under the mouflon closest to me, and caused him to fall. Of course, this caused the other one to fall as well. The problem with that particular tactic was that they fell right on me. Consequently, now I was lying on my back in the dirt, with over three hundred pounds of kicking and fighting mouflon rolling all over me.

I succeeded in getting out from under the bottom mouflon, and I lay down on top of him to hold him down. I realized that I would have to take the top mouflon and rotate him in a complete circle, right over top of me, to get them untangled. Oh, by the way, these two mouflons were not simply lying there calmly, they were kicking and fighting at about the same pace as when they were on their feet. I was on the belly side of the mouflon on the ground and he was kicking me with all four feet.

The mouflon on top had his back to me, but I knew as I pulled him over me, to get him unscrewed, I would be exposed to his feet as he went past me. I was determined to make my move as quickly as possible. I grabbed the top mouflon by the belly, and tried to pull him over me. He was so heavy that I couldn't get him elevated enough to slide over me. I tried again, and failed.

At this point, I was having serious doubts about my decision making skills. What in the heck did I think I was doing. There were many times in the animal business (As you have no doubt learned.) when I wondered just exactly who was making the decisions that came out of my head. I figured there must be some sort of tiny, maniacal, masochist living in my head, giving me bad advice. Never-the-less, I had made this stupid decision, and my stubbornness forbade me from giving up.

As we were struggling there in the dirt of the mouflon section, we had managed to get ourselves in a position so that our backs were downhill. I thought that this might give me the additional leverage I needed to get the top mouflon up and over me. I made one last ditch pull, and the top mouflon slid up onto my chest. I adjusted my grip, and got my hand up under his back, so that I could continue to push him over me. In the mean time, the mouflon on the bottom was still doing his best to take my clothes off with his hooves.

I pulled fast and hard, and ducked my head into the body of the lower mouflon, as I pushed the flying legs of the top mouflon over me and around past the lower mouflon. I was hoping that the motion of the bodies was having the desired effect on the locked horns, because I was too busy with bodies and legs to be watching the horns. The unscrewing worked. As the top mouflon slid over the bottom mouflon, their horns came loose, and the top mouflon took off like a shot.

When the bottom mouflon saw the top mouflon run off, he redoubled his efforts to escape. I was only too happy to oblige. So, amid a host of flying hooves, I rolled off the bottom mouflon. He jumped up, and was off like a rocket without so much as a thank you. Oh well, the animals rarely thanked me, but the feeling I got from knowing I had performed a service for them was reward enough.

I got up, dusted myself off, and hobbled down to the boat. I still had animals to take care of. I still remember the sting of that clear, fresh water on my raw hands as I bent to wash the dirt off of them. I splashed a little water on my face, hopped in the boat, started the motor, and off I went for another exciting day in the animal business.

# Afterword

I would like to thank Norma Romeo and J. Keith Gulledge for their editorial help which was so sorely needed.

# About the Author

The author currently lives in Ocala, Florida with his wife, Yvonne, and son, Larry, and an old dog named NIMH. He is currently teaching Chemisty at a local high school. He enjoys spending time with his granddaughter Brittany, reading, computer gaming, and thinking about those "good old days."